THE GENIUS

HOWARD BRENTON

The Royal Court Writers Series
published by Methuen
in association with the Royal Court Theatre

To Jane

A METHUEN PAPERBACK
First published in Great Britain as a Methuen Paperback original in 1983 by Methuen London Ltd, 11 New Fetter Lane, London EC4P 4EE and in the United States of America by Methuen Inc, 733 Third Avenue, New York, NY 10017, in association with the Royal Court Theatre, Sloane Square, London SW1.
Reprinted 1985

ISBN 0 413 54650 0

Without chaos, no knowledge

Paul Feyerabend

The Genius was first performed at the Royal Court Theatre, London, on 8 September 1983, with the following cast:

LEO LEHRER, *a professor of mathematics*	Trevor Eve
GILLY BROWN, *a student of mathematics*	Joanne Whalley
RICHARD WEIGHT, *a university vice-chancellor*	Clive Swift
GRAHAM HAY, *a university bursar*	Hugh Fraser
VIRGINIA HAY, *a statistician, married to Graham*	Anna Nygh
ANDREA LONG, *a student*	Alyson Spiro
TOM DICKS, *a student*	Paul McGann
CLIFF JONES, *a cycling lecturer*	Alan David
A SKELETON *playing the violin*	Sue Latimer

Directed by Danny Boyle
Designed by Peter Hartwell
Lighting by Gareth Jones
Sound by Patrick Bridgeman

ACT ONE
Scene One: The Prize-winner
Scene Two: Equations in the snow
Scene Three: Theories in a wood
Scene Four: Crisis in a garden

ACT TWO
Scene One: An accident
Scene Two: State moves
Scene Three: Treacheries
Scene Four: Embassy
Scene Five: Peace moves

ACT ONE

Scene One: The Prize-winner

A blackout.

A low electrical hum. The hum rises slowly to a thunderous noise. The noise rises in pitch to –

A second of silence.

Then with a loud, sharp explosion a blue flash crosses the stage in mid-air, giving the audience this retinal image –

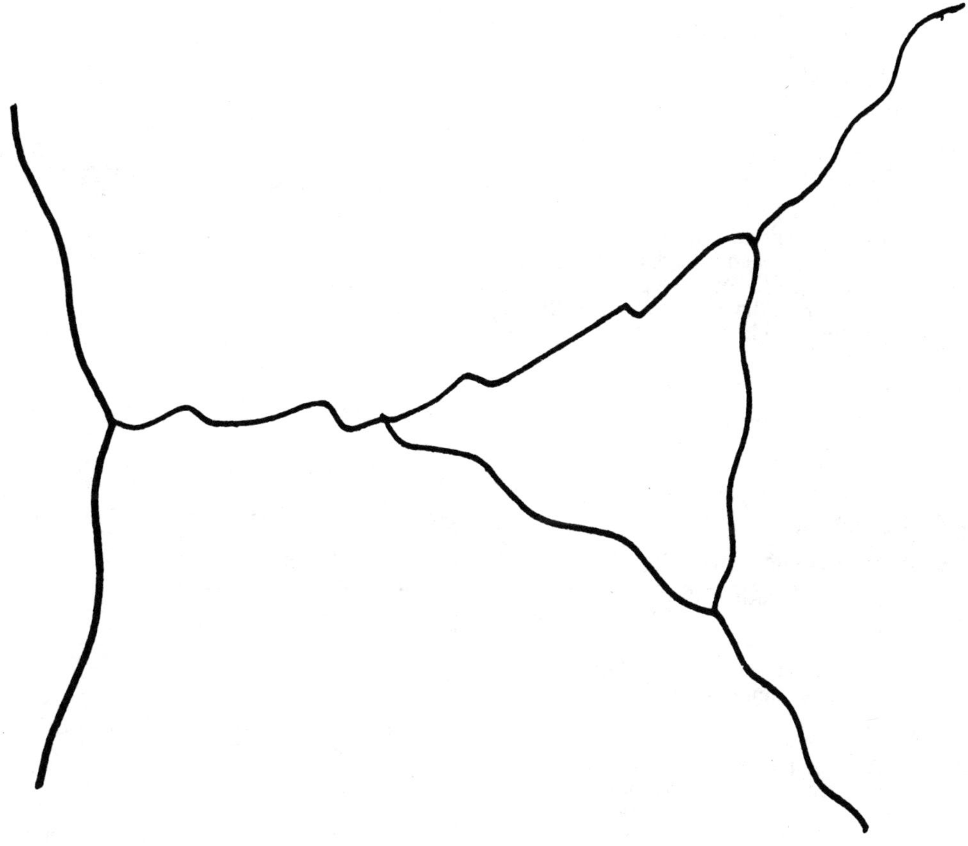

After the flash, in the blackout, the sound of wind and rain. The lights come up slowly.

Campus grass.

A rainy, windy, grey early autumn afternoon.

A small, pink umbrella, turned inside out, is blown onto the stage.

LEO LEHRER *walks on. He is thirty-six. He holds the lapels of a short jacket to his throat.*

LEO: Exile. To an English university in the Midlands. Jesus, look at it. The edge of the Holy American Empire. Concrete in rain.

GILLY BROWN *runs on for the umbrella. She is eighteen. She carries a large, old brown suitcase. She drops the suitcase and runs to the umbrella, which she picks up.*

GILLY: Do you know where E-Block is?

Nothing from LEO. *She tries to put the umbrella to rights.*

My Mum's. She's had it twenty years. First time her daughter leaves home, what does she do, warn me about the wicked world? No, she gives me her pink umbrella. I'll have to tell her on the 'phone tonight it's bust. She'll cry, I know. The waterworks. Do you know where E-Block is?

LEO *stares at her.*

Well thank you. Thank you very much.

GILLY *picks up the case and goes off.*

LEO: Exile.

He looks about him.

Late twentieth century style. The Romans used to send their bad boys – lovers of the Emperor's wife, dirty poets – off to little islands. Maybe they did the same for their scientists.

He laughs.

A Roman engineer gets ahead. Invents the steam engine, two thousand years too early. The emperor has him dragged before him, in chains. 'OK Albertus Einsteinus,' says the emperor. 'Steam engines do the work, whadda the slaves do? You wanna wreck the empire's economy? You wanna get us all killed? So long, smart guy, enemy of the state. Go sit in a puddle and count your abacus in Lowland Britain.'

He puffs his cheeks and blows out.

Jesus, am I jet-lagged.

RICHARD WEIGHT, *aged sixty-two, the* VICE-CHANCELLOR *comes on with* GRAHAM HAY, *aged forty-five, the* BURSAR. The VICE-CHANCELLOR*'s hat is blown across the stage.*

VC: My hat!

The VICE-CHANCELLOR *and* GRAHAM *laugh.* LEO *runs at the hat and catches it with a forward roll, skilfully coming to his feet again.*

GRAHAM: It's Leo Lehrer.

VC: Really?

The VICE-CHANCELLOR *fumbles glasses suspended round his neck from beneath his coat and peers at* LEO.

So that is the radical and mathematical young lion. Doesn't look much. I'd better do the honours.

GRAHAM: I'll introduce you.

GRAHAM *goes towards* LEO, *hand outstretched.*

Leo. You got to us early.

LEO: Hello Graham.

GRAHAM: We weren't expecting you 'til next week.

LEO: I got itchy. Got on a flight.

GRAHAM: This is a good chance. Leo, this is Dr Richard Weight, the Vice-Chancellor of the university. Vice chancellor, Dr Leo Lehrer.

VC: Who has my hat at first slip.

LEO: What?

GRAHAM: Cricket.

The VICE-CHANCELLOR *and* LEO *shake hands,* LEO *limply.*

VC: I followed all the too and fro-ing. Getting you out of the Massachusetts Institute of Technology was like staging a robbery of Fort Knox.

His joke falls flat. Polite smiles. LEO *wants to withdraw the hand, the* VICE-CHANCELLOR *does not.*

Forgive me if I be the cat that's licked the cream. But vice chancellors the length of the land will tear out their eyes when they know we have a Nobel Prize-winner.

LEO *turns away.*

LEO: A third. A third of a Nobel Prize. And we were lucky.

VC: Ah, the collective 'we'. Never the personal 'I'. We measure out our lives in democratic verbal twitches. Even in academic life there are trots. But we chairpersons stumble on, squelching in our consensus wellies.

LEO (*to* GRHAM): What are wellies? What are trots?

GRAHAM: Rubbers and trotskyists.

LEO: My God.

VC: I must tread the mud of committee language, the dreary art of saying nothing so that only the right people know what you mean. So – you lighten our darkness, Dr Lehrer! The trots will go mad to hear it and I get blood in my administrative wellies – but, in the end, the glory of a university is the exceptional, individual brain. The individual human being.

LEO: Shucks.

GRAHAM *shakes his head at* LEO.

VC: There will be a more formal do to welcome you. But since we've bumped into each other let me say I hope you take part in the general hurly-burly of campus life. Birmingham is a car drive away, but that city is hardly the Florence of the English Midlands. So we amuse ourselves. I have a little thing in mind. A vice-chancellor is a gargoyle set in the concrete architecture, but underneath I am an Arts Man. Shakespeare was my field. Did an image count. On average Shakespeare has 24.7 images every hundred lines, twice that of any of his rivals. Not many know that. Anyway – here is my little thing. Why don't we give a public talk together? We'd take a general theme – 'The nature of creativity', nothing too taxing. Do it in the Arts Centre. That's –

He points.

The monstrosity with the pop art tower. They're always desperate for something to put on over there. I even thought of a title – 'The marriage of Art and Science?'

A silence.

LEO: Mr Vice Chancellor.

VC: Dick –

LEO: Dick.

He pauses.

All I want from you is computer time That's what got me here. Computer T–I–M–E. Written in my contract. OK celebrate, you landed a Nobel Prize-winner. Go print a picture of my arse on top the unversity note paper. You want anything more – call my lawyer in New York.

A silence.

VC: Tea-time. We are on our way to the Senate House. Join us? The first muffin of autumn?

LEO: Go fuck yourself.

GRAHAM (*low*): Leo, calm down!

VC: Well. See a lot of you, no doubt. When you're settled in.

Nothing from LEO.

Exit pursued by an American bear. My hat?

LEO *gives the* VICE-CHANCELLOR *the hat.*

But think over our public talk. 'The marriage of Art and Science.'

The VICE-CHANCELLOR *nods and smiles and walks away with* GRAHAM, *who glances at* LEO *angrily.*

LEO: Vice-Chancellor!

The VICE-CHANCELLOR *and* GRAHAM *stop.*

They got divorced. When Galileo sold out to the Inquisition in 1633. Three hundred and fifty years ago. Didn't you notice?

The VICE-CHANCELLOR, *not smiling, turns away again.*

VC: The radical and mathematical young lion is a prickly little shit.

GRAHAM: I'll pour oil.

VC: You had better. You twisted all our arms to get him. Hope he's worth it.

He goes off. GRAHAM *hesitates then goes to* LEO.

GRAHAM: What are you trying to do? You may be a film star of the academic world but there's no need to come on like Jane Fonda on a Vietcong tank.

LEO *is looking away.*

Leo?

LEO: Who are they, over there? Students?

GRAHAM *looks.*

GRAHAM: Oh. No. Townies.

LEO *doesn't understand.*

Kids from the city. They come up and bum drinks in the student bars. There are thefts and there are fights. But – this is meant to be a people's university.

LEO: Some o' Britain's legendary unemployed, eh?

GRAHAM (*calling out*): Er – on the path, please.

A silence.

The path.

A VOICE, *off.*

VOICE: Fuck off!

GRAHAM *looks away with a sigh.*

LEO: Hey Graham, we are on the grass.

GRAHAM: But we are members of staff.

LEO: Got you.

GRAHAM: Leo, this may not be the time or place. But when you want to say something serious in England it never is the time or place.

He hesitates. LEO *turns and looks at him.*

LEO: OK, OK, Graham, burst all over me.

GRAHAM: I feel I got to know you while we were negotiating your famous contract. And you well know that is a hell of a contract – copper-bottom protection for a programme of pure research. Fine. Fine. We all pay lip service to pure research, in a university 'being for pure research' is like being for life and against death. But actually we loathe it, because we all know, in our tiny souls, that real mathematics, science, pure knowledge aspires to the condition of music. And a university is paid for – by a government that wants weapons, a car industry that wants the petrol-free engine. And who is going to fight a war or run a car on a bloody string quartet? It doesn't concern you and I don't want it to concern you, but I nearly went to the wall to get you here. Don't be fooled by the VC dribbling on about muffins: university officials are professional politicians, their apparent senility is a rhetorical ploy. The VC can talk about blood in his administrative wellies, mine are full of broken toes. If I go down you will need that fabulous New York lawyer.

LEO, *a shrug, hands held out.*

All right all right! I can handle the politics. I know who is carrying knives in the university Senate against your professorship. I will strangle their togas around their old-school ties. You will never know the murder that was done on your behalf. That's my life! I go to many meetings, to me an agenda glitters with razor blades. I look at my fingers making notes on a report and know they are podgy. Nervous over-eating is a bureaucrat's disease. But I persist. You see, though I am embarrassed to say it, I believe in the university. Learning. Free thought. Not a factory for careers but a place for true, human experiment. So! I could do with a little – grace, Leo. Not for me personally, but for some grist to throw into the wheels within wheels. A little human grace? After all, we are the angels. Our cause is purity.

LEO: Purity.

He laughs.

You got any idea what you been stripping your stomach wall for, Graham? You got any idea what my research is?

GRAHAM: Unified Field Theory?

LEO: Yeah? And what is that?

GRAHAM: You want me to blind myself with your science? I'm just another arts graduate, with a PhD on the more boring bits in William Blake. It's up to you to know what you're doing. Presumably you do know what you're doing?

LEO: Yes. Or no. Or – too much.

He laughs.

No calculation is pure, Graham, no calculation is pure. Mathematics, the mother of machines and bombs?

GRAHAM: Leo –

He hesitates.

Around MIT, when I was over haggling for you, there was a rumour. Hardly anything – just the rattle of ice in the dry martinis. But it was hinted the reason MIT were willing to let you go –

He hesitates again.

LEO (*low*): Oh Jesus.

GRAHAM: Vague, it was very vague, but it said you soft peddled on something. A project, financed by the Pentagon? And that, by letting you come to us, you were being punished.

LEO (*low*): Jesus.

GRAHAM: Is there anything, Leo?

He pauses.

That I should hear?

LEO: What do you want to hear? OK you've been sold a dud, 'old chap'. My lack of human grace is brought on by a dose of the post-Einstein clap. Real guilt and dread. I had the new E equals MC squared but flushed it down the john. I feared it would burn the world. But Spiderman crashed in through the men's room window, dived down the pan and rescued the magic maths for the Pentagon. That kind of thing happens all the time at the Massachusetts Institute of Technology.

GRAHAM: Why is the American sense of irony like a kick in the head?

LEO: No irony. I am kicking you in the head.

GRAHAM: The rumour was true? You refused on some work?

A silence.

Can you tell me what it was?

LEO (*shouts*): How the hell could you understand it if I did?

A silence.

Sorry. I'm sorry.

He laughs.

Wrote about little lambs, didn't he, William Blake? How the hell can a poem about a little lamb equip you to understand the mathematics of modern physics?

GRAHAM: It may, morally.

LEO: Bullshit.

GRAHAM: Yes.

A nervous laugh.

The great divorce.

During LEO*'s speech* VIRGINIA HAY, *aged thirty-nine, comes on.*

LEO: Don't worry, Graham. I am intact. You'll get what you paid for. Your hick computer is going to wonder what has got it by the balls. I am still an all-American boy – give me ego and fame and money and get me laid. What do I do about a screw around here, by the way?

GRAHAM: Whatever you do, don't touch the students. You can bite off more than you can chew.

VIRGINIA *has seen them. She comes downstage.*

Oh, darling.

LEO: Hello.

GRAHAM: My wife, Virginia. Virginia –

VIRGINIA: Leo Lehrer. I've seen your photograph.

LEO: I hear we tread the same muddy pool.

VIRGINIA, *with a glance at* GRAHAM.

VIRGINIA: Yes, I was a mathematician. Before I gave birth to children. Statistics. Behavioural psychology.

LEO: Counting rats in mazes, ringing bells?

VIRGINIA: That kind of thing.

GRAHAM: Leo's dodged having tea with the VC.

VIRGINIA: A coward.

GRAHAM: But must come to supper.

VIRGINIA: Must.

GRAHAM: Really Leo, anywhen. Just drop round.

VIRGINIA: Ring the bell.

LEO: I'll do that.

GRAHAM: Um –

He looks up, raising his umbrella.

Rain again.

VIRGINIA *joins him under the umbrella He puts an arm about her waist.*

Welcome.

LEO nods, looking down. GRAHAM and VIRGINIA turn and walk away.

He's stoned, he's stoned, I know he's stoned.

They go off. LEO pulls his jacket up above his head, his arms held out by the tightened sleeves. CLIFF JONES, aged fifty, comes on, riding a bicycle. He wears cyclist's yellow bad-weather clothing, his head is bare. He sees LEO.

CYCLIST: Bloody awful weather. But, on the other hand, we could all be dead. See you.

He cycles off. LEO begins to spin slowly. At the back two students, ANDREA LONG and TOM DICKS come on. They carry leaflets. TOM has his beneath a coat. GILLY comes on, still carrying her suitcase and umbrella.

GILLY (*to* ANDREA and TOM): Scuse me. Could you tell me where E two-six-eight is?

TOM: Student Residential Block E. Door two. Floor six. Room eight. Is – that hunk of concrete.

He points.

Not that hunk, not that hunk, but that hunk.

GILLY: Thanks. I've been wandering about.

ANDREA: First year.

GILLY: Yes –

ANDREA: You're soaked. Come and have coffee in the Union. Then we'll take you over to E-Block.

TOM, looking at the spinning LEO.

TOM: Who's that idiot?

ANDREA: Don't know. I'll do him. (*To* GILLY.) Don't go away.

ANDREA goes quickly to LEO.

TOM (*to* GILLY): You too.

He takes the leaflets from beneath his coat. It is a large sheaf and disordered. He hands GILLY a selection.

For a happy start to university life, get your left-wing literature down you.

GILLY: Oh. Thanks –

ANDREA (*to* LEO): Oy. You in there.

LEO stops spinning. She holds out a leaflet. He does not take it.

END.

LEO: EN what?

ANDREA: Campaign for European Nuclear Disarmament.

A silence. Then LEO sinks to his knees giggling. He speaks gutturally.

LEO: Nuc – lear – Disarm – a – ment. Nuc – lear Disarm – a-ment.

ANDREA: CND? 'Ban the Bomb'?

TOM: Come on, Andrea!

ANDREA (*to* LEO): What's so funny?

LEO gestures her toward him. He points. She looks where he is pointing then back at him.

?

LEO: Spiderman!

He rolls over, foetus-crouched, laughing.

ANDREA: Get lost.

GILLY, holding the leaflets out to TOM.

GILLY: I don't want anything to do with politics. I'm here to study mathematics.

A moment still – GILLY holding the leaflets out to TOM, ANDREA holding the leaflet out to the rolled up LEO. A blackout.

Scene Two: Equations in the snow.

Snow. Brilliant light. Gog Hill. Boxing Day. GILLY wanders on. Like everyone else in this scene she is wrapped up against the cold. She wears mittens. She carries the pink umbrella, furled. She also carries a loose-leaf binder under her arm. She tramps downstage, preoccupied. She stops.

GILLY: 'Fury said to a mouse
That he met in the house
Let us both go to law; I will
prosecute you –'

She opens the loose-leaf binder and looks at it. Then snaps it shut. Then speaks the second verse, drawing mathematical symbols with the tip of the umbrella in the snow.

'Come I'll take no denial:
We must have a trial;

For really this morning I've
nothing to do.'

The CYLIST *comes on, puffing. He carries his bicycle over his shoulder.*

CYCLIST: Merry Christmas.

GILLY *stares at him.*

Don't think I'm mad, climbing a hill in the middle of a field with a bicycle on my back. My eight year old son is down the bottom. He bet me I couldn't ride my bike down Gog Hill on Boxing Day. So here I am. Didn't think it would bloody snow.

GILLY *stares.*

Well. Here I go.

He runs with the bicycle across the stage, mounting it at the last moment. A silence, then a distant yell, that fades. GILLY *waits, then looks back at the snow. She writes with the umbrella again, the equations spreading across the stage.*

GILLY: 'Said the mouse to the cur
Such a trial dear Sir,
With no judge and no jury would be
wasting our breath.'

The VICE-CHANCELLOR *walks over the hill. He has a large, knobbly walking stick.*

VC (*humming*): Pom pom pom, pom-pom pom pom.

He sees GILLY.

Merry Christmas.

He waves his stick in the air to the tune.

Pom pom pom. Bach's 'Musical Offering'. The great theme, layer on layer. Balanced. Pom-pom pom pom.

GILLY *stares.*

You are?

GILLY: Gillian Brown.

The VICE-CHANCELLOR *is stranded.*

First year maths.

VC: Ah. Happy with work and play?

GILLY: Don't know –

VC: Boxing Day beer for me. Over Gog Hill to the pub, far beyond. Know what this little hill is?

GILLY: Yes.

He ignores that.

VC: A Norman keep. Wholly artificial. But before that, a Roman fort. See!

Stick pointing.

The Fosse Way, great Roman road – the jugular artery of Roman Britain, running through the fleshy Midlands to go 'blip' and dodge around this bump. No doubt the hill was here before they made the road. A Celtic site. Before that, a Neolithic burial mound? Layer on layer! Balanced! And on top the snow, the cowpats and us.

GILLY *stares.*

On now. A pint of Greene King by lunchtime.

He waves the stick.

Work and play.

He goes off. GILLY *takes off a mitten and gets a ball-point pen from a pocket. She writes in the binder.*

GILLY: 'I'll be Judge, I'll be Jury'
Said cunning old Fury:'

She looks up, thinking. Then –

'I'll try the whole cause and condemn
you to death.'

ANDREA *half walks, half runs on. She is in the middle of a row with* TOM, *who runs on after her. He carries a half-drunk litre bottle of cheap red wine.*

TOM: But why? Why resign?

ANDREA: Because I'm tired, bored, sick and tired, tired, tired – of men shouting at me about the Vanguard Party.

TOM: What a deeply, deeply –

He shouts.

Stupid remark.

ANDREA: There, you shouted at me!

TOM: You can't resign. No one resigns, they just change sides. We're all locked in a room together. There's only one way out and that's called death.

ANDREA: Oh thank you, thank you. One more male thought to make me feel bad. (*To* GILLY.) Hello.

GILLY: Hello.

GILLY *continues to look at her binder.*

TOM: You've not got into Rad. Fem. anti-marxism. Not that.

ANDREA (*to* GILLY): What do you think?

GILLY: A lot. But not all the time.

TOM: Jesus Christ! If I were an ideological agent working for the CIA trying to invent a creed to fuck the Far Left, I think I'd dream up Rad. Fem. anti-marxism. Divide the socialist camp down the old sex war lines. Get at the reds in their beds. Andrea, infantile, bloody infantile –

ANDREA: Oh! Oh! Infantile. Trigger word. 'Cos Lenin said it, didn't he. 'Infantile disorders'. Only Lenin meant anarchists, you mean women. I do believe communism to be sharing, dignity, the hope of the world – but why does it look like a conspiracy of men? Very old men, on a balcony, with all the guns and all the police. Vanguard Party?

GILLY: Get off!

ANDREA: The English revolution in male mouths begins to sound to me – just like football. Something men shout about down the pub, getting into the class war and the Greene King. Big cocks and big ideas, killing people.

GILLY: Get off my sum!

ANDREA: What?

She looks.

Oh. What is it?

GILLY: Told you. A sum.

TOM: I mean –

He waves the bottle.

Universal education! Literacy!

ANDREA (*to* GILLY): Do I know you?

GILLY: I'm first year maths.

ANDREA: Yes?

GILLY: I met you first day of term. You gave me a leaflet. Don't you remember?

ANDREA: Sorry.

TOM, *turning, the bottle held high.*

TOM: The ghosts of Chartists, old socialists and reformers, haunt the concrete university. They gave their lives so we could read. And what is the most read magazine in the Students' Union? The *Beano*. Back in your graves, comrades.

He wanders backwards into GILLY*'s figures.*

We are good, middle-class children, squandering two hundred years of socialist agitation –

GILLY: Get your feet off!

TOM: What?

ANDREA: You are trampling on her mathematics!

TOM: ?

He looks down.

Oh.

GILLY: Go away. You talk too much. Clack clack. That's all I hear from people like you. Clack clack. So go away.

TOM: There you have it! Authentic, pig-headed, ostrich in the shit heap, anti-intellectual apathy.

ANDREA: Ostrich with a pig's head?

TOM: I know, I know, the wine's run out, the metaphors are mixed and I need the pub.

He jumps clear.

ANDREA (*to* GILLY): He thinks International Capitalism is making him an alcoholic.

TOM: Right!

He cartwheels.

Ph! Come my mid-twenties, will I still do that? Andrea. Pub. Please.

He backs away.

A pint of Green Worker, then.

ANDREA *and* TOM *eye each other. Then he turns and runs off.*

ANDREA: Don't think too badly of us, Ms Workhead. Think, what if we're right, we left-loonies, and there is a 'Great It' running our lives? Down to you doing one and one are two in the snow.

GILLY: You're still talking.

ANDREA *nods, backing away.*

ANDREA: OK.

She smiles.

Just don't work too hard for the bastards.

ANDREA *turns and walks off quickly.*

GILLY: Work. Words. Clack.

She holds the binder between her knees and demonstrates with her hands.

There are no layers. Only one thing, passing through itself. You think you see different things – there, there and there. But – blink blink blink. It's just one thing you've seen, one force, one whole –

She is dead still, in mid-sentence.

Oh, I can do the work but I can't do the words. Clack clack!

She turns her hands over and stretches them above her head.

After six – no, it's weekend rates on Boxing Day – anyway, I'll ring my mother and tell her I've done a really good bit of work. And she'll have the waterworks. 'Why didn't you come home for Christmas, first time ever not, you're making Daddy ill.' 'I told you, Mum, I'm doing this work I – I – I've got to do this work.' 'No I'm not on drugs, no I'm not catching VD with a man, I'm doing a calculation! A sum! And you'd clash with it you see, Mum, your voice, you, the way you fill up the air, the look on your face, that funny little hair on your nose, it would all go out of my head because the sum is very beautiful and you – are – so – very – ugly. Mum.'

Her arms flop down, the binder slips from between her knees. For a moment she is still, then she brightens.

Oh well! Pick yourself up and dust yourself off.

She picks up the binder and her umbrella, opens the binder and wanders away.

Wish I had a new binder, this one's getting chewed up.

She goes off. The stage is empty for a moment, then LEO *and* VIRGINIA *come on. They walk slowly, relaxed, six feet between them, hands in their pockets.* LEO *spins once, looking around.*

LEO: Is Graham –

VIRGINIA *points into the distance.*

VIRGINIA: A dot upon the white. Talking to the vice-chancellor. A little university politics in the snow. Like a little dog 'Oh look. The VC is in that field, walking to the pub' and he's off, all waggy tail.

LEO: My flesh crawls when you bad mouth him.

VIRGINIA: Shall I tell him about us?

LEO *stops walking, she continues.*

LEO: OK.

She stops.

Tell him every time he looks the other way you screw his best friend.

VIRGINIA: OK.

They look at each other. Then they laugh.

We are not great and good lovers. It would be wonderful if we were, but we are not.

LEO: No way.

VIRGINIA: He's off to Paris next weekend after all. The UNICEF Conference – on the world shortage of school textbooks.

LEO: Why don't they just spend the money on the books?

VIRGINIA: Why protest? We can go to bed.

They look at each other.

It's still the school holidays. I'll send the children to his mother.

LEO: You are a ruthless woman. I look Graham in the eye in the Staff Club and think – don't you know your marriage is kind of damp? Like in bed with come from me and your wife?

VIRGINIA: Don't try to shock me, Leo. I've given birth to two children, I'm nearly forty and married to an Englishman who loves his mother. I can't be shocked. I am at a dangerous age. Either I live it or I don't.

Suddenly she is upset.

LEO: Hey Virginia –

VIRGINIA: No!

She tries to laugh.

I do keep on having baths. I'm terrified he'll smell us.

LEO: You Europeans begin to get to me. Can't you people have a good time without pain?

VIRGINIA: Pain in love is a great European tradition.

LEO: Learn the trick from the American way of life – don't give a shit. Once you don't give a shit you can be kind, gentle, whatever you want. Just like –

He clicks his fingers.

That. Don't give a shit.

VIRGINIA: All right. Let's make love in the snow.

A silence.

LEO: Why not? Babylon is my home town.

They hesitate. Then giggle. Then he goes to her and rumples up her skirt. She counters by pulling at his trouser belt.

Look, er –

VIRGINIA: Don't worry. I've decided to be a sucker for experience.

She pushes his trousers down.

LEO: Virginia, we going to do this?

He looks around.

Britain is a densely populated island.

VIRGINIA, *sitting down on the snow, pulling off her tights.*

VIRGINIA: What's the matter, Mr American Macho? Can't you live it?

Her tights catch on her boots. She tears them from her heels and throws them away. She sits back, looking at LEO.

LEO: Oh shit.

VIRGINIA: Shit you too, citizen of Babylon.

LEO: Ok! Ok.

He pushes his trousers down his legs. They catch on his shoes. He falls over in the snow.

Jesus Christ it is cold!

VIRGINIA: Come on.

She holds her arms out. He squirms in the snow, kicking his trousers off. He crawls to her. She turns him over and lies on him.

LEO: Hey. Wow. We getting into birch twigs later?

VIRGINIA *kisses him lightly.*

VIRGINIA: Leo – why –

A kiss.

Aren't you –

A kiss.

Using the computer?

LEO: All this and you want pillow talk too?

VIRGINIA: I was over there, Christmas Eve. They said there's been no work from you since you got here, at all.

A kiss.

Zero.

A kiss.

Zilch. What do you do all day, Leo? When you're not taking the jeans off some little student?

A finger on his lips.

You stare at the wall, don't you. Leo, your clothes smell of hash. Your eyes drift. You soften.

She caresses his hair.

You are rotting away.

LEO: It's like this.

He pauses.

I feel, I feel – like a snowball's been rammed up my arse –

He rolls over. They fight and laugh.

VIRGINIA: Leo –

LEO: Come on, let's go all the way, let's strip –

They roll pulling at each other's clothes.

VIRGINIA: You've got to start working.

LEO: I am, sex and science – a new equation of the flesh –

VIRGINIA: Calculate again, Californian –

She pushes snow up his shirt front.

LEO: Hey! Wow! Ow!

VIRGINIA: Madness, madness oh madness –

They have rolled to where GILLY *wrote in the snow. He sees the figures. He is dead still.* GRAHAM *walks on. He, too, is still.*

GRAHAM: Is it me? Something about me? Personal, something in me, you want to destroy?

VIRGINIA (*to herself*): It has happened, it

has happened.

GRAHAM: Some mannerism of mine?

LEO: Who did this?

GRAHAM: Something private, something deep, that you hate?

LEO *stands.*

LEO: Who did this?

GRAHAM: That you want to tear out, dig out of me, my bowels and burn them?

VIRGINIA: Graham, very, very quietly, just – go away.

GRAHAM: What if I'd come up the hill with the VC? What? How could we go on, I –

LEO (*to* VIRGINA): You do this? Some crazy practical joke? You sneak out in the snow and get me up here, and aim to ball me on it, give me a lift, a bad time, all the nightmares?

VIRGINIA: What are you talking about?

GRAHAM: I suppose we're going to be adult about this! Bloody, bloody adult!

LEO: That!

He runs up and down the equations, still with his trousers off.

VIRGINIA: What is it?

LEO: You don't know?

VIRGINIA: No.

With a finger she points through the figures.

GRAHAM: I'm spinning. It's my life. What about the children? What about me?

LEO: Only a fragment of it but it's right! It's right!

VIRGINIA: A fragment of what?

LEO: What I ran away from, there in the snow.

He scans the landscape, shouting.

Who are you? Come on! Show yourself!

VIRGINIA, *still at the figures.*

VIRGINIA: Amazing.

LEO *kicks the figures away in the snow.*

LEO *kicks into the snow, destroying the equations.*

LEO: It's on snow, on grass, on a hill.

VIRGINIA: Leo –

LEO: Water and ice. It goes. It'll mulch back down, mud and grass. Hey, but –

VIRGINIA: ?

GRAHAM: ?

LEO: Aerial photography!

VIRGINIA: ?

GRAHAM: ?

LEO: Something drawn on snow! That leaves an impression on grass? Like archaeology? See it, on the ground? We got to burn this, bonfires –

He scrabbles at the snow and earth.

Rake the ashes, dig it in, dig it in –

He stops, crouching, head down. He begins to shake.

Oh God, God.

GRAHAM: I wait for someone to make a remark to me. I don't expect an apology, an insult will do.

VIRGINIA: Shut up Graham, you're pathetic.

GRAHAM: Thank you, darling.

Near tears.

You're so kind, so kind.

He floods with anger.

(*To* LEO.) You bastard!

LEO: Who cares?

GRAHAM: You say something to me?

VIRGINIA: Please, it is Christmas.

GRAHAM: I said, you say something to me?

LEO: Who cares? Join in 'old man'. Let's all screw ourselves into the surface of the planet. What's it matter, when the whole globe, ye olde spaceship earth, is going to burn?

He laughs. A gesture at the churned-up patch of snow.

We're all going to burn, shouting at each other about who fucks who.

GRAHAM: You two-bit ageing hippy. I trusted you and what do you do? Cock your leg up on everything, my trust, my marriage. I'm going to kick your teeth in.

LEO: Old fellow, I am in better shape than you –

GRAHAM *falls on* LEO, *who hits him in the stomach. They roll grunting.*

VIRGINIA: For Godsake stop it! You're intellectuals. The humanist tradition and look at you –

GILLY *runs on. She stops.*

GILLY: How many more of you?

They stop fighting and look at her.

Coming up, messing me up.

LEO: You –

GILLY: It's not fair. Lucky for you I've got it written down, in my binder.

She walks, then runs off.

LEO: Hey!

He tries to stand but GRAHAM *holds his leg.*

Virginia, get her!

GRAHAM *bites* LEO*'s leg.*

You stupid bitch, get her!

GRAHAM *bites* LEO*'s leg again.*

Ow!

He hits the back of GRAHAM*'s neck.* GRAHAM *grunts and loosens, unconscious.*

VIRGINIA: You hit him in the head.

LEO, *shouting over the landscape, turning.*

Come back! There's more! There's more! Come back, I'll show you!

VIRGINIA: You hit him in the head!

LEO: You know her? That little girl, that little fool, you know her?

A silence. They stare at each other.

Don't you understand? The ground has opened up under my feet.

VIRGINIA: You bastard. How can we be safe from people like you?

Still for a moment. Then a blackout.

Scene Three: Theories in a wood.

A wood. Moonlight. LEO *and* GILLY.

LEO: Gillian.

GILLY: Hello.

A silence.

LEO: Had to bullshit my way into the university Senate House to find you.

GILLY: Oh? Why?

LEO: The files. You know they've got a file on every student over there, with a photograph?

GILLY: I got my 'photo done on Euston Station, one of those machines for passports. Behind a little curtain. You worry drunks are looking at your knees. I'm talking too much 'cos you're famous.

A silence. She takes the binder from beneath her coat.

LEO: Is that it?

GILLY: Maybe.

LEO: Can I look?

GILLY: Why don't you want me to show it to anyone? And why write me a letter, why not come round to E Block?

LEO: Have you shown it to anyone?

GILLY: And getting me out here. Daffodil wood. This place had got a bad reputation.

LEO: Have you shown the equations to anyone?

GILLY: No, actually.

LEO *puffs his cheeks and blows out.*

LEO: Where you from, Gillian?

GILLY: Watford.

LEO: What's Watford to go and warp the universe?

GILLY: A place.

LEO: You still want the City of Watford to turn with the planet? You still want there to be a planet?

GILLY: Don't know.

LEO: You don't know.

GILLY: I don't know what you're talking about –

A cycle bell rings. The CYCLIST *rides on, the lights on his bicycle shining over the stage.*

LEO: Get down.

GILLY: What?

LEO: Off the path.

The CYCLIST *gliding past.*

CYCLIST: Evening boys and girls in the bushes. Snow has gone, soon be bluebells. Take precautions, don't get pregnant.

He rings the bell and has gone.

LEO: Who is that guy? I see him in the staff club. He drinks eight pints of beer a night.

GILLY: Don't know.

LEO: Creepy.

They are still squatting. He puts out a hand. She is still, then she hands him the binder. He opens it, takes a flashlight from his pocket and reads. He turns one page, he turns another.

A solo violin begins to play the theme and three part invention from Bach's 'The Musical Offering'.

The stage darkens to a blackout. LEO *and* GILLY *still squat,* LEO *reading the binder by flashlight.*

Toward the back of the stage a SKELETON *glows faintly. It is playing a violin.*

The SKELETON *becomes brighter, the music louder, rising to a fearful pitch of distortion.*

The SKELETON *lifts the bow, sharply. A second of silence.*

An explosion as the

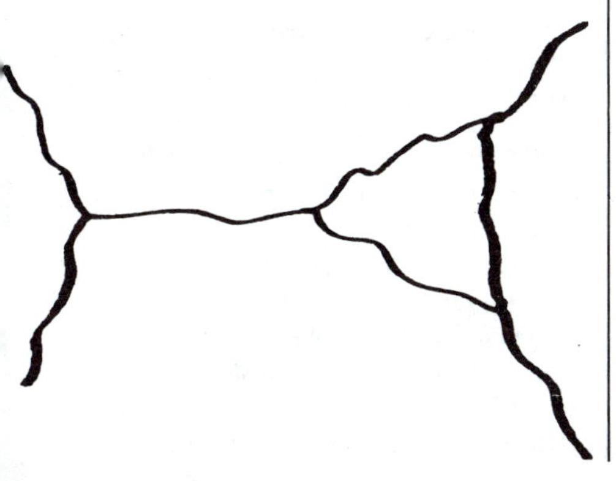

flashes across the stage.

The SKELETON disappears. LEO *reads on.*

Slowly the moonlit wood returns to the stage.

Then LEO *switches the torch out and closes the binder.*

A silence.

LEO: All right. Where did you steal it?

GILLY: What do you mean?

LEO: Off one of your teachers?

A silence.

GILLY: No!

LEO: Who then?

GILLY *shakes her head.*

Some smartarse graduate? What, he screw you? You pick this off the bedroom floor and walk out with it, to give him a lift?

GILLY: Why do you think a man had to write it?

LEO: A woman then –

GILLY: Why not? A woman, a beautiful woman, with beautiful thoughts –

LEO: You saying this maths spewed out of some kind of lesbian scene?

GILLY: You've got a sick mind.

LEO: Whoever did this –

He slaps the binder.

Has got the sick mind.

GILLY: It's brilliant!

LEO: Who wrote it, Gilly? Give me her, give me his name.

GILLY: Me! Me! I did, said Gillian, with my little – I did.

Both still for a moment. Then LEO *flips open the binder, takes out a pen and switches on the torch. He scribbles.* GILLY *looks away, upset. He finishes then pushes the pen and binder at her. He tosses her the torch, contemptuously.*

LEO: Answer that.

GILLY: A test?

LEO: Yup.

GILLY: Get lost.

GILLY *glares at him but then puts the binder on the ground, angrily. She holds the torch and looks at what he wrote, sucking the top of the pen. Then she writes fast, at length. She stops abruptly, looking at it, then pushes the binder, pen and torch into his lap. He looks at it.*

LEO: Jesus fucking Christ.

GILLY: It's not like being St Joan and hearing voices.

She laughs.

Angel coming down and telling me what to write. Well, not exactly!

She thinks, then –

It's more like knowing a piece of music by heart, without ever having heard it before, or read the notes. You just sit down at the piano, play and the air remembers the music, and there it goes, out of the window.

She laughs.

No, music you can play wrong, wrong key, it jars. Music's got something inside it that says it's right or wrong. But maths hasn't, has it? It's the funniest thing about it. You can't prove logically that maths is logical!

LEO: Godel's inconsistency theorem.

GILLY: Yes.

LEO: When did you understand Godel's theorem?

GILLY: When I was about nine.

LEO: Nine.

GILLY: I didn't know what it was called then, of course. Didn't have the books! Enid Blyton is a bit thin on the philosophy of mathematics.

LEO: When you were nine, you understood the fundamental inconsistency of mathematics.

GILLY: Why not? There a law against it?

LEO: How do your teachers handle you? Arc welding mask and asbestos gloves?

GILLY: Oh, I don't let on.

LEO: How d'you mean?

She shrugs.

GILLY: I do bad work deliberately. Just enough, so they won't realise.

LEO: Why do that, Gilly?

She shrugs.

Because it scares the shit out of you?

GILLY: No!

LEO: It does. I know the signs. The 'take this cup of sick from me' look in the eye.

GILLY: I'm just frightened at being so good at it. Hang over from your school, I s'pose. Y'know, in school, you get a reputation for being weird, liking books or something, and you get your head put down the toilet. I think that goes on, out of school too. You can get called a fraud, or people tell lies about you and twist everything you do. Mess it.

She pauses.

Like when you know a beautiful tune and someone sings it horribly. So horribly, the tune sounds rubbish.

LEO, *looking away.*

LEO: What you trying to say, you're some kind of fucking artist?

GILLY: I'm brilliant at mathematics. I didn't ask to be, but I am and that's that. What I believe is, when we're born, we know everything. All maths, all science. We can't say it, we can't really think it, it's an 'isness' – is, is, *wis*dom, you see it when a baby looks at you. A baby in a pram is happy being alive, happy with – oh, the earth going round the sun, happy with genes wriggling in our cells, happy with things about nature the adult world won't discover for a thousand years, if ever – happy.

LEO: 'Til it shits itself.

A silence, GILLY *glaring at him. Then she snatches at the binder.*

GILLY: Give it to me.

He wrenches the binder away, standing.

You'll twist it, you'll – it!

He throws the binder away, upstage into the darkness. He pulls his jacket up around his head and spins.

LEO: The cradle is full of shit, Gilly. Oh boy, you have not a blind idea of what you have done.

GILLY: Tell me then, big American.

He stops spinning.

LEO: What do you want? Me to teach you? I don't want to teach. Grin to the class, in pretence that all is fine and in harmony? All the teaching you need is – go away and blow your mind to bits, little girl.

GILLY: What did you get me out here for then?

LEO: Bad conscience. No, too fancy. Terror Gillian.

He pauses.

Terror.

GILLY: Of what, Mr Nobel Prize-winner?

LEO: OK.

He pauses.

OK. OK. It is time to teach, it is time to pass the poison on.

He pauses.

You got any physics?

GILLY: Didn't do physics at A level. It's numbers I love, physics – ugh. All metal and iron.

LEO: Oh sister, you really are some kind of child of nature. Out o' some kind of backwoods of the world called Watford and you have written out – the pure mathematics – for the unity of the four forces of nature.

GILLY: That what I done? News to me.

LEO: OK student. Four forces of nature, what are they?

GILLY: Earth? Air? Fire? Water?

He laughs.

LEO: Medieval honey, medieval. Still, teacher must not despair. Even Isaac Newton believed in magic.

He rips off his jacket.

I give you the first force of nature –

He bundles his jacket into a ball and throws it up. It falls before him. With a mock bow.

Gravity. Attraction of two bodies, my jacket and me to the planet. Infinite in range. The binder of stars. Nothing escapes it, not a feather, not the planet Saturn, not you not me, not a particle of atomic dust, drifting in space.

He picks up the torch.

The second force of nature.

He switches the torch on.

The electrical force. Binds atoms to atoms in molecules, gives light out the socket for your TV – lightning, God in the sky?

He flicks his finger.

Come here. C'mon! Get your pop science down you, you want to know how the ugly old world is made.

He grabs her round the waist, holding her tight.

The strong nuclear force. Binds the nucleus of the atom. Give me your bag.

GILLY: What?

LEO: Your shoulder bag.

GILLY: You want some funny business mister, I'll scratch your eyes out.

LEO: Fourth force of nature. Weak nuclear force.

They spin, he whirls the bag around their heads.

Holds electrons! To the nucleus of the atom!

GILLY: Ow!

LEO: Wonders of nature! Force on force! Brutality in balance, harmony o' good old fucked creation –

GILLY: Bastard!

She gets a hand free and hits him on the side of the head, they stumble and fall. They roll and then sit up.

LEO: Shucks we just had a nuclear explosion.

GILLY: That your idea of teaching? With hate?

LEO (*low*): What are the four forces of nature?

GILLY *at once.*

GILLY: Gravity. The electrical force. The strong nuclear force. The weak nuclear force.

She pauses, then again effortlessly.

Gravity, the attraction of bodies with any weight?

LEO (*low*): Mass.

GILLY: Mass. The electrical force, binding atoms in a molecule. The strong nuclear force, binding the nucleus of the atom. The weak nuclear force, binding electrons to the nucleus.

She shrugs.

So?

LEO: So, Gillian.

He pauses.

So under the farmlands of Illinois, there is a machine. Fermilab. It is a tunnel, in a circle, four miles wide, along its rim magnets of enormous power. A circle around which they smash bits of atoms. A particle accelerator. Europe has one, outside Geneva, so big it swings across the border into France. The Soviets have one, in Serpukhov, Siberia. The only secrets are nature's, the only secrets are nature's.

He laughs to himself, then continues.

Millions of dollars, millions of roubles to smash bits of matter near the speed of light, round and round under the grass. Looks kind of innocent – mankind playing on the beach with grains of sand. That is how it is presented to the public – for the love of it, the love of knowledge. That's how you talk about your maths, Gillian, like it's love.

He pauses.

But the machines in Illinois, Geneva and Siberia are not for love. In this world, millions of dollars and roubles are not spent for love. They – are – spent – for – power. What they want to do, is prove that the four great forces of nature are, in truth, one force.

He pauses.

To see them as one force. In truth.

GILLY *to herself, demonstrating with her hands as in Scene Two.*

GILLY: Like you think you see different things, there, there and there. But – blink blink blink. It's just one thing you've seen, one whole, one –

She hesitates on the word.

Force.

LEO: What's the matter, sister? Suddenly seen a gleam of darkness in the middle of all that light?

GILLY (*to herself*): Patterns.

She holds up her hands, fingers splayed, one behind the other.

If you can see two different patterns, the right way round –

She reverses a hand.

You see one pattern.

LEO: Yup! It's called the Gauge Theory.

GILLY: I know all about that, mathematicians have been doing that stuff since the nineteenth century.

LEO: Yup! We been doing all kinds of stuff, for centuries. Like we are all programmed? All rushing to one great rational conclusion? Like by force of brain, becoming God? Early in 1983, in the Geneva machine, they did one million experiments, to prove that the strong nuclear force and the weak nuclear force, are one and the same.

He pauses.

Thirteen times out of the million, they got it right.

GILLY: It's enough. All they need now is the mathematics.

He turns on her.

They need the mathematics, student! Time and time again some mathematician sits down and for the sake of purity, love? Writes out some elaborate pattern. Hell, when we work out what quarks are, the mathematics were those of a Frenchman, Evariste Galois, who wrote down all his ideas the night before he was killed in a duel in the eighteen eighties. Like you, sitting down in the snow, one Christmas vacation?

GILLY: But it's wonderful.

A silence.

What I wrote could help scientists?

A silence.

You had better tell me why it's not wonderful.

LEO: Albert Einstein said that, if he had known that his 1905 paper on Special

Relativity was to lead to the atom bomb, he'd have given up mathematics –

GILLY
LEO (*together*): And made cuckoo clocks –

GILLY: Didn't though, did he! Come on teacher, 'teach'!

LEO: I'm cold.

He wanders over to his jacket and puts it on as he speaks.

I did the same work in America. It hit me like it hit you. Pur – it – y. The world in a grain of sand, under your fingernail? I had all that innocence. Arrogance.

A silence.

Then I was on a beach. Californian holiday? Up came an individual and sat down beside me. Blue eyes, the body of a surfer. The Government, Gilly, the Government of A – mer – ik – a. And it began.

GILLY: What did?

A silence.

LEO: Everything. The threat in a smile. The offer of power. A lead role in a cage.

He puffs his cheeks and blows out.

They wanted the work and they wanted me, for Uncle Sam, the free world, for weapons research, for – a – bomb. That's what it means, the tune you and I scrawled out with our ballpens. You describe how something lives and dear old human kind will use your words to kill it.

He shakes his head.

Oh boy, the consequence of describing life is death?

He laughs.

I am not a hero, I am an American boy who wants to get fucked. I was made for fame and sex not paranoia in a lonely room, out of my mind that the 'phone is bugged. So I said – OK, no calculation is pure. Therefore calculate no more. I gave up, Gilly, I closed down, I exiled me into my own head. If you are shit scared of the damage you can do, do nothing, eh?

A silence.

In the end they let me alone. And let me hide, here in England. Then you walked out in the snow one morning.

GILLY: But you can't not think.

LEO: No? Try it.

GILLY: A thought is a thought. You can't not have it –

LEO: Don't you know how fucking naive that is? How fucking young?

GILLY: No I don't!

She looks at her hands.

The – equations are as natural as –

She searches for the phrase.

A tree. If a murderer ties someone to the tree and kills them, or if lovers lie down and make love under its leaves, the tree doesn't care! And if men with blue eyes in America do something horrible with the equations – I don't care. I can't. What I think is me and what I write is me and that's that. And you've not stopped thinking, have you? Closed down on the outside, but inside, you can't stop, can you? And you didn't tell them, the blue-eyed men. You're even a hero, though you don't want to be. You can't stop it, you can't stop nature –

LEO (*shouts*): Right! Right! Little Miss Light from the cradle, happy on Mother Nature's tit.

He runs into the darkness and comes back with the binder.

I'll show you, I'll show you.

He opens the binder on the ground.

Look! Look!

She kneels down and opens the binder. They work.

Birdsong. The stage begins to brighten. Dawn, a fine sunny day. The shadows of trees and branches across the stage.

They finish work. GILLY *closes the binder. They are very cold.* LEO *stands and shakes his clothes. He offers* GILLY *a cigarette, lights it for her. They smoke.*

GILLY: That's how they'll do it.

LEO: Yup.

GILLY: It's only – thirty sheets of paper. Like watching you – build up – crazy towers, a mile high from it. All metal and iron.

LEO: Yup.

GILLY: Bomb. Bomb.

LEO *takes a deep breath, breathes out.*

What do I do? Have breakfast? I don't think the egg on the plate will look the same. Ring my Mum? 'I know how they can make a new generation of weapons, Mum! Isn't that wonderful?'

She smokes. She laughs.

OK. Let's burn it.

LEO: 'Til the next –

GILLY: Bright kid from Watford, yes. We got it wrong, haven't we, there must be something wrong in the physics –

LEO: You got the physics all the way.

GILLY: Just two clever shits like us?

LEO: You'll go over it all the time. Welcome to insomnia, sister.

GILLY: Just play the piano. The air will know the tune. But I can't now. The tunes will burn the air. It's unfair! Doing maths – was a joy.

LEO: Galileo said one day, scientists will come forward overjoyed with a new discovery to be greeted with a universal cry of horror.

GILLY (*giggles*): Another clever little shit, was he?

They pause.

Do you want to do it?

LEO: You.

She throws back her head, takes a deep breath and lets out a long scream, quiet at first but rising.

The birdsong swells. The lights fade as the Bach theme is heard.

Scene Four: Crisis in a garden

A summer garden. Sunlight, dappling the stage. A table covered by a white cloth, upon it opened bottles of wine and wine glasses.

All wear bright summer clothes –

But for GRAHAM, *who is in a pair of trousers from an old suit, sandals without socks and a dirty white shirt, sleeves rolled up. He is discovered walking upstage to the table. He picks up a bottle. He looks at the label.*

VIRGINIA *comes on.* GRAHAM *does not see her.*

GRAHAM: Are we all now to drink Californian wine?

VIRGINIA: What to some is truth, to others is a drink of piss.

GRAHAM: True, true.

He pours a glass, puts the bottle down and turns. They look at each other.

VIRGINIA: I didn't know Leo had invited both of us. Otherwise I would, or would not, be here.

GRAHAM: G – g –

VIRGINIA: What?

GRAHAM: Gang bang!

VIRGINIA: Sorry?

GRAHAM: Maybe that is what he has in mind.

VIRGINIA: Graham –

GRAHAM: Summer party? End of term. It is warm. The sun is at its highest arc above the English Midlands. The young we seek to teach come to a zenith in their lives. Career dreams and dreams of love, lock. Now middle-aged lecturers hope to find themselves naked with their students in high, green bedrooms.

He sips wine.

VIRGINIA: Why are you stuttering?

GRAHAM: I'm n – not.

VIRGINIA: You can't go on, sleeping in the caravan, parked slap in the middle of the campus!

GRAHAM: A touch of squalor in the academic paradise.

VIRGINIA: The university won't put up with it.

GRAHAM: I am the university, I'm the bloody b – bursar.

VIRGINIA: All right, go potty. But beware – the English love eccentrics, but turn on them when they become insanitary.

GRAHAM: Don't worry. I go over to the staff club to use the gents.

VIRGINIA: I need a drink.

GRAHAM: How –

NEXT AT THE ROYAL COURT THEATRE
730 1745

From 27th October

THE GRASS WIDOW

by
SNOO WILSON

Directed by MAX STAFFORD-CLARK
Designed by PETER HARTWELL
Lighting by ROBIN MYERSCOUGH-WALKER

the cast includes
RON COOK and TRACEY ULLMAN

SNOO WILSON's new play is set on a snake infested dope farm in Southern California. The marijuana is ready for harvesting and there are conflicting claims on the real estate.

THE GRASS WIDOW is an honest and witty look at Californian life in the material world and its implications for all of us.

ROYAL COURT THEATRE UPSTAIRS
730 2554

TWO PLAYS BY SARAH DANIELS
The current holder of the George Devine Award

We are delighted to present 2 plays Upstairs by the current George Devine winner, Sarah Daniels, whose bleak and hilarious RIPEN OUR DARKNESS played to capacity houses in 1981.

THE DEVIL'S GATEWAY is a fast funny and forceful play about guerilla warfare in Bethnal Green while MASTERPIECES is a hard canny look at how pornography infiltrates our lives.

MASTERPIECES comes to us following its successful run at the Manchester Royal Exchange.

THE DEVIL'S GATEWAY
Directed by ANNIE CASTLEDINE
Designed by ANNIE SMART

with
CHRISSIE COTTERILL, PAM FERRIS, ROGER FROST, SUSAN PORRETT, LIZZIE QUEEN, RITA TRIESMAN

From 7th October

And

MASTERPIECES

Directed by JULES WRIGHT

the cast includes
EAMON BOLAND, SHIRLEY DIXON, WILLIAM HOYLAND, PATTI LOVE, KATHRYN POGSON

THE ROYAL COURT THEATRE
presents
The World Premiere of

THE GENIUS

by
HOWARD BRENTON

Leo Lehrer A Professor of mathematics	TREVOR EVE
Gilly Brown A student of mathematics	JOANNE WHALLEY
Richard Weight A University Vice-Chancellor	CLIVE SWIFT
Graham Hay A University Bursar	HUGH FRASER
Virginia Hay A Statistician,married to Graham	ANNA NYGH
Andrea Long A student	ALYSON SPIRO
Tom Dicks A student	PAUL McGANN
Cliff Jones A cycling lecturer	ALAN DAVID
Skeleton playing a violin	SUE LATIMER

ACT ONE

Scene One	THE PRIZEWINNER
Scene Two	EQUATIONS IN THE SNOW
Scene Three	THEORIES IN A WOOD
Scene Four	CRISIS IN A GARDEN

INTERVAL

ACT TWO

Scene One	AN ACCIDENT
Scene Two	STATE MOVES
Scene Three	TREACHERIES
Scene Four	EMBASSY
Scene Five	PEACE MOVES

First performance at the Royal Court Theatre on 8th September 1983.

Directed by	DANNY BOYLE
Designed by	PETER HARTWELL
Lighting by	GARETH JONES
Assistant Director	SIMON CURTIS
Sound by	PATRICK BRIDGEMAN
Production Manager	ALISON RITCHIE
Stage Manager	RUTH HOGARTH
Deputy Stage Manager	GILL FOX
Assistant Stage Manager	STEVE BRADY
Wardrobe Supervisor	PAM TAIT
Front of House Manager	RICHARD MASTERMAN
Casting Director	GAIL STEVENS
Production Photographs	JOHN HAYNES
Poster & Leaflet Design	NEVILLE BRODY
Press & Publicity	MIN JONES
	SHEILA FOX
	(730 5174)

THE
ENGLISH STAGE COMPANY
AT THE ROYAL COURT THEATRE

THE COUNCIL
President:
Mrs Neville Blond OBE
Chairman:
P.H. Newby CBE

JRS Boas
Stuart Burge CBE
Anthony C.Burton
Harriet Cruickshank
Allan Davis
Robert Fox
William Gaskill
Mrs Henny Gestetner OBE
Derek Granger

THE ENGLISH STAGE COMPANY was founded in 1956, principally to present the work of new writers at the Royal Court Theatre.

This theatre operates the Regional Theatre Trainee Director Scheme in Association with the Independent Television Fund.

David Hare
Jocelyn Herbert
David Kleeman
Lady Melchett
Joan Plowright CBE
Greville Poke
Rob Ritchie
Lord Snowdon
Pam Tait
Sir Hugh Willatt

Josephine Bannerman	Cleaner
Gary Barlow	Housekeeper
Gill Beadle	Youth Worker
Danny Boyle	Director,Theatre Upstairs
Patrick Bridgeman	Sound
Peter Bull	Eve.Stage Door
Simon Byford	Tech.Manager, Theatre Upstairs
Jennifer Clarke	Membership Sec & YPTS Administrator
Simon Curtis	Trainee Director
Joan Emmett	Wages Clerk
Stephen Evans	Box Office Manager
Sheila Fox	Press & Publicity Manager (730 5174)
Chris Harding-Roberts	Master Carpenter
Sally Harris	Box Office
Leona Heimfeld	Secretary
Toby Ingham	Assist.Electrician
Anne Jenkins	General Manager
Carol Johnson	Stage Door/ Telephonist
Cathie Jones	Wardrobe Assistant
Ivy Jones	Cleaner
Terry Jones	Financial Assistant
Richard Masterman	House Manager
Betty McGauran	Cleaner
Robin Myerscough-Walker	Chief Electrician
Louise Page	Resident Dramatist
Christopher Pearcy	Box Office
Gilly Poole	Literary Assistant
Alison Ritchie	Production Manager
Rob Ritchie	Associate Director
Hilary Salmon	Financial Administrator
Tim Spencer	Dep.Master Carpenter
Max Stafford-Clark	Artistic Director
Gail Stevens	Casting Director
David Sulkin	Director,Young People's Theatre Scheme
Pam Tait	Costume Supervisor
Christopher Toulmin	Dep.Chief Electrician

ROYAL COURT THEATRE SLOANE SQUARE SW1 Box Office 730 1745 T.U.730 2554
Admin 730 5174

VIRGINIA: Don't ask me how the children are, don't, or I'll scream.

GRAHAM: Do –

VIRGINIA: No longer. Our American sexual Odysseus has begun to work hard. He rows with the computer people day or night. He is also, day or night, with a little student from E Block. Didn't you know?

GRAHAM, *a quick shake of the head.*

GRAHAM: Out of t – touch.

He pauses.

Can I get you that drink?

VIRGINIA: No.

GRAHAM: Don't want – near me?

VIRGINIA: I'm afraid you'll smell.

Lower.

Smell.

GRAHAM *pulls at his shirt sleeve, looks at it, then sniffs his armpit.*

GRAHAM: Sexual Odysseus?

He nods.

He's cruel too. See, he's put us in his garden and changed us into p – pigs.

He walks away. VIRGINIA *looks away, then goes quickly to the table and pours herself a drink.* ANDREA *and* TOM *come on.*

Hello Tom. How's Trotsky?

TOM: Pissed off, bursar. How's caravaning?

GRAHAM: Smelly.

TOM *laughs.*

Don't you laugh. You too will come to middle age, bad teeth and arm-pitty shirts.

TOM: Not me, bursar.

GRAHAM: Expecting early death?

TOM: Why not?

GRAHAM: By nuclear holocaust or by alcohol?

TOM: Get stuffed, Graham.

GRAHAM: I've tried that. Tried that.

TOM (*to himself*): Fucking hell.

TOM *goes to the table and picks up a bottle of wine and drinks from it.* VIRGINIA, *giving* ANDREA *a glass.*

VIRGINIA: I shouldn't know and I shouldn't tell you. Do you want to know?

ANDREA: I sort of know, anyway.

VIRGINIA: You got a first.

ANDREA: Yes.

VIRGINIA *sips her wine.*

VIRGINIA: What will you do? Stay on and do an MA?

ANDREA: I am going to work as an orderly in a mental hospital.

VIRGINIA: I see.

ANDREA *sips her wine.*

For the young or old?

ANDREA: How do you mean?

VIRGINIA: I don't know much about it, but I imagine the old and insane are really disgusting.

ANDREA: It is a hospital for old people.

VIRGINIA: The men must be worst.

ANDREA: There are men.

VIRGINIA: The sexual drive of insane, old men. A real purgatory for a young woman with a first class degree. You make me very angry.

ANDREA *sips again and says nothing. The* VICE-CHANCELLOR *comes on. He carries a shooting stick.*

VC: Ah junketing, junketing. To slurp the cup of summer.

TOM (*to* ANDREA): Uh uh, the heavy mob.

GRAHAM: Oh! Vice-Chancellor!

The VICE-CHANCELLOR *ignores him, planting the shooting stick and sitting on it. He looks around and chooses* VIRGINIA *to talk to.*

VC: Virginia, my dear.

VIRGINIA: Hello Richard.

He kisses her on the cheek.

VC: Is mine host to be seen? I rang the doorbell but there was nothing, so round I came to the garden.

VIRGINIA: Yes, where is Leo?

VC: Nice to see you here with Graham.

VIRGINIA *takes a step back.*

VIRGINIA: Red, white or rosé?

GRAHAM *is shaking his head, moving his hand, as if talking to himself. The* VICE-CHANCELLOR *looks over at him. Suddenly they are all looking at him.*

VC: It is extremely tedious, Virgina, when senior members of the staff will not keep their bodies under control.

Nothing from VIRGINIA.

A glass of white, please.

TOM: A glass of wine, a glass of class, a nod a nonce. The English intelligentsia are in their garden.

ANDREA: Oh shut up.

She turns away from him.

TOM: No sweat, 'doll'! The flowers grow. Anything wild and wonderful is called a weed and pulled up by the root. Red moles under the lawn are dug out and gassed, the turf put back, smoother than before. All the little talents are in a row in the sun, happy with their prizes. Sprayed to kill off any harmful insects, y'know, the odd marxist idea? So sip, sip! Never mind the wind is American and, just over the hedge, there are bodies on the barbed wire. (*To himself.*) In a way, I like it, in a way it is right. It is what I know. Believe what you want, do what you want, we are all licenced killers walking among the flowers. Well I am, I am.

TOM *swigs from the bottle. As he spoke a bundle of papers, print-outs and notebooks,* GILLY*'s binder among them, bound with a big red bow and flowers has been lowered down above them, jerkily.*

GRAHAM: There's something coming d – down.

They all look up.

VC: Ah. Rag time?

ANDREA: It's from the tree.

VC: I do believe the string leads to that window.

GRAHAM: He's right. It goes over a nail.

VIRGINIA: For Godsake.

She shouts.

Leo!

TOM: What is all this?

He goes to the bundle. GRAHAM *stumbles to the bundle, pushing* TOM *aside. He ruffles through the papers, helplessly.*

GRAHAM: It's mathematics.

VIRGINIA *takes the papers from* GRAHAM *and walks away with them, her back to the company.*

VC: Party game? Clues, paperchase, crock of gold at the end?

GILLY *walks on. She is horribly burnt all over her body, the burns fresh. She is hairless and naked but for a few traces of charred rags. She is blind, her eyes bloody pits. She carries a silver tray, upon it champagne glasses, filled. They all stare at her.*

TOM: Er –

GRAHAM, *a loud giggle.*

GRAHAM: Hahahahahahaha!

A silence.

VC: What a pity no one told me it was fancy dress.

GILLY *turns aimlessly, stumbling, the champagne glasses chinking.* VIRGINIA, *reading upstage, sinks silently to her knees.*

ANDREA (*to* GILLY): What do you want us to do?

TOM: Looks like champers.

He strides to the tray. He takes a glass, drinks liberally from it, holds the liquid in his mouth for a second then sprays it out and bends double.

Ahhh!

LEO *walks on.*

LEO: We did her up, best we could, first degree burns? The epidermal layer, what we call 'our skin', gone? The blood vessels beneath, exposed? And blinded, if not by the flash, by photothalmia? Ultra-violet light? The ozone layer stripped away, ten minutes outside, and – eyes gone?

VC: Ah!

He slaps his thigh.

CND. Touch of street theatre? Very jolly.

TOM, *holding his throat.*

TOM: Ahhh!

GRAHAM: What was in the glass?

LEO: Hydrochloric acid one, twenty megaton bomb on Birmingham, that is something like what it would do to us, in this garden.

GRAHAM: For crying out loud he said he drank –

LEO: Hydrochloric acid, so what, the worst we can do to each other? Serve acid in a garden, nothing, twenty megaton bomb, nothing, there is more horror to human intervention than we can dream.

All still for a second. He shouts.

Dream!

GRAHAM: B – b – b – b – b – bloody irresp – p – p – p – p – ponsible –

ANDREA: Get a drink of water!

She runs to the table. The VICE-CHANCELLOR, *rising from his walking stick.*

VC: If this is to go too far, if you have gone too far –

LEO: Ok, it is not HCl, no one's throat will burn and Gillian, that is a swim hat, paint on it, not a burn from the flash fire of Birmingham, England, nuked.

TOM: And I tell you that weren't fucking champagne.

LEO: A little human piss with Alkaseltzer for the bubbles.

TOM *swigs at the wine and splutters.*

TOM: I mean why me?

LEO: Why anyone of us, man?

VC: Your champagne turns out not to be hydrochloric acid, merely urine. We must be grateful for small mercies. It is the end of summer term, one tolerates the odd collapse into bad taste. Nevertheless, perhaps an explanation? The university does expect more from its Nobel Prize-winner than a glass of pee – with or without bubbles.

VIRGINIA, *still kneeling, laughs.*

VIRGINIA: Love it, love it, I love it. Oh you clever bastards of the world.

She stands, the bundle in her hands.

You are very bright and golden, Leo, and you? (*To* GILLY.) A little girl fresh from her comprehensive, lit up like a light bulb and wrote it in the snow? (*To* LEO.) For you to fall over. I love it. The great leaps of science, Copernicus, Newton, Einstein and the last great leap? A low farce.

GRAHAM: But what? What have they done?

VIRGINIA: Nothing a mathematician with a good, first class degree, could not grasp. (*To* GRAHAM.) But have you got a degree in mathematics? (*To the* VICE-CHANCELLOR.) Have you? (*To* ANDREA.) You? (*To* TOM.) You? No. Good, educated people, with no hope of ever knowing how the world is made. That's part of the farce.

TOM: Elitist bullshit. What are you, a priesthood, with secrets to hide?

VIRGINIA: That is what we are. (*To herself.*) I tried to leave, denounce my vows.

She lets the bundle of papers and notebooks fall to the ground.

VC: The young man has reason. I am an Arts man. The simplest long division and I go down with brain fever. But I have a layman's picture of the atom. Little balls going round big balls? Therefore explain, explain!

GILLY: There –

She pauses. They all look at her.

There are four forces of nature.

LEO *puffs his cheeks and blows out. Then –*

LEO: What are they? Someone answer before the bell goes clang.

ANDREA: Earth, air, fire, water?

VIRGINIA: Clang.

LEO: Would that not be beautiful? Back in the middle ages, yes, the world was made of earth, air, fire, water. But for us?

GILLY, *sing song.*

GILLY: The four forces of nature are the strong nuclear force, the weak nuclear force, the electrical force – and gravity.

LEO: When we say force, put no pictures in your head. There are no pictures. What you see in the pop science programmes on TV, atoms like (*To the* VC.) your balls going round balls – forget it. All the pop science is propaganda, to say all's right with the world and Mother Nature loves us. There are no pictures of existence, Mother Nature is blind.

GILLY: What Albert Einstein tried to do, for forty years, after he did what made him famous was write –

She pauses.

Write a series of equations, uniting – the four forces of nature into one. One force, one whole. He knew that if he did that, it would be like writing out – the secret name of God.

LEO: Einstein didn't make it because the schmuck was a moralist. He wanted to believe in God too much, the eye in the sky. He threw up when the mathematics wanted to say 'Blind, it's blind'.

He pauses.

I am no a moralist, I don't give a fuck. I sat down and wrote out the equations in America. That.

He points at the bundle.

And I looked upon all my works and – threw up. I ran. Hid. Tell them why, Virginia.

VIRGINIA: Any mathematician sees it at once.

GRAHAM: Oh G – God, they said at MIT. (*To* LEO.) M – m – military work? Classified material? That is c – c –

LEO: Yeah yeah, what the Pentagon wanted, Captain America will be zapping out a' the trees any moment now.

GRAHAM, *free of the stutter.*

GRAHAM: Leo! The grossest irresponsibility, abuse of academic behaviour, all trust –

ANDREA (*to* VIRGINIA): A bomb.

VIRGINIA: 'Yup'.

TOM: Yip, yippee –

LEO (*to* GRAHAM): It's trust we want from you. All of us in this garden, like it or not – we are the children of Galileo. And look what the old bastard's given us to handle. Ok! Gilly's tried to do the shock stuff, let me try the reason. Here we are, teachers and students. Help two of your number deal with the product of their – twisted, bloody, clever clever brains. Protect us. Help us deal with what we've done. Be a university.

GRAHAM: Vice-Chancellor –

VC: Yes, I think I have to intervene, would the undergraduates present please leave, there may be a matter for Senate here –

GILLY *throws the tray down on the ground, smashing the glasses.*

GILLY: They'll never understand. They'll twist it. They'll destroy it. They're stupid, they're all dead.

She scoops up the bundle of papers in her arms.

It's – time – we – got – out – of – the – pram.

All freeze for a moment. Then GILLY *turns and runs. A blackout.*

ACT TWO

Scene One: An accident

Night. The path through the wood. The CYCLIST *rides on, lamps lit. He rings his bell.*

CYCLIST: Out my way foxes, out my way, little furry animals!

GILLY *runs on still in the make-up of the garden, straight at the* CYCLIST. *She knocks him and the bicycle over. They both go sprawling. He sits up.*

My clips. One's popped off. I don't want to lose my clips.

He looks at her.

What in heaven's name have you done to yourself?

GILLY: They say you're a communist.

CYCLIST: I beg your pardon?

GILLY: That's the gossip. 'Mong the students.

CYCLIST: Nothing broken.

The CYCLIST, *standing.*

GILLY: They say you go to Moscow.

CYCLIST: Cast as resident red mole am I?

GILLY: See, I thought 'write it on the walls, stick it on trees' – or let it run down drains, in the sewers and in the rivers, out to sea, washed up on beaches, all gluey, stuck in sea gulls' feathers, or! Throw it in reservoirs, let it come out the taps and everyone drink it, like a drug!

CYCLIST: Goodness. Everyone drink what?

GILLY: The secret of the world.

CYCLIST: You working up a fever?

GILLY: But now I think 'Give it to Russia'.

CYCLIST: A high old fever. Better get you to the student's nurse, hot drink and wrap up.

GILLY: No listen, what the traitors did, with the atom secrets? Maybe they'were right and heroes.

CYCLIST: Kim Philby and Co., heroes of the revolution? I always thought they were a bunch of upper-class wankers. Here, have my coat.

GILLY: No!

CYCLIST: Now you listen to me. All you are is a stupid, spoilt, know-nothing child, messing about in a wood. Knock me off my bike, prattle about communism? You want to go to the Soviet Union, take a package holiday. Can you stand?

GILLY *backs away.*

GILLY: You're like all the rest. Crows on the wire, on the barbed wire fence. All the teachers, all the mums.

CYCLIST: Don't run off!

GILLY: I want to tear your eyes out. Blind you. So you don't see me, so you sit on your fence blind and never see what I do, what I see.

She runs off.

CYCLIST: Come back here! Oh buggeration, buggeration.

He gets on the bicycle and rides off. The stage darkens. In the distance POLICE *with lights and a dog, barking.* VOICES *calling –*

VOICES: Gilly! Gilly! Gilly!

Scene Two: State moves.

A small room. The VICE-CHANCELLOR *and* GRAHAM. *The* VICE-CHANCELLOR *in a luxuriously covered armchair. A drinks cabinet, in the wall.*

VC: Any sign of her?

GRAHAM: No.

VC: Looked on the Senate House roof? Students on the blink often go up there, to throw themselves off. Half a dozen in my time. I talked them all down, but for one. He is now a paraplegic, in Cheltenham. Sends me a card every Christmas.

GRAHAM: We've searched the roofs.

VC: One ends up hating the young. The endless repetition of telling them what the world is like. The waiting for them to believe it when they're thirty.

He pauses. GRAHAM *shifts.*

And the American? Presumably in a narcotic haze somewhere?

GRAHAM: The police say he left the search and went home.

VC: With your wife?

GRAHAM, a little jerk of the head but says nothing. The VICE-CHANCELLOR *drums bad-temperedly on the arm of the chair.*

Running, running.

GRAHAM: I'm sorry?

VC: This business, running away, out of our hands. Events are in train. As an administrator I have always disliked 'events'. In a big institution, it is an essential condition for progress that nothing happens.

He stops drumming and stares at GRAHAM.

How long have you known that I'm dying?

GRAHAM: I –

VC: Come on! We discuss matters of high state. Let's not waste time over my disease.

A pause.

GRAHAM: Eighteen months.

VC: What, sneaked a sight of my medical report? A nod to a secretary, the slide of a filing cabinet drawer and behold – cancer.

GRAHAM: Richard, I am really horribly sorry.

VC: Be horribly glad! You are ambitious. Pour me a scotch.

GRAHAM: Should you?

VC: Oh fuck you, fuck you rotten!

GRAHAM *pours him a drink and hands it to him.*

It is late at night, let us be naked. I want you to be Vice-Chancellor of this university. Not some clapped-out Tory ex-minister, come to cut everything in sight. I have groomed you, I have conspired for your cause. You have not helped. The wobble in your married life.

GRAHAM: I am through that.

VC: And now our wayward American.

GRAHAM *pauses.*

GRAHAM: Yes.

VC: It's down to you. You got him here, you watered him, now you –

A gesture.

Snip him off. Preferably at the root.

The VICE CHANCELLOR *slouches back in the armchair, the whisky to his lips.*

Train him up the wall. With all the other colourful personalities.

GRAHAM: It may not be a matter of personality.

VC: I lose faith in you, Graham – everything is a matter of personality.

GRAHAM: There are great causes.

VC: Nonsense. There is only self-interest. Self-interest is another phrase for 'being alive'.

GRAHAM: That's cynical.

VC: Not cynical at all. Honest. Graham, after all the American has done to you in your private life, I do believe you still want to be a martyr for his science.

GRAHAM: He is a bastard. But – a bastard who is trying to talk about whether or not we are going to blow ourselves to bits.

VC: Nonsense again. He is talking about the size of his own ego.

GRAHAM: The nuclear holocaust isn't a matter of a personality disorder.

VC: That is exactly what it is. CND? Ban the Bomb? The whole thing is a middle-class neurosis that is in danger of becoming hysterical.

GRAHAM: Richard, in the Science Block of the university you and I run, there are smartarse graduates dreaming of stripping genes from the nuclei of human cells –

VC: Don't slander my Science Block. That is my pride and joy. That Science Block gets this bloody place funded.

GRAHAM: But to do what? There are mathematicians over there calculating how to fracture matter itself. We administer that, we mild, decent men. We administer the nuclear holocaust.

VC: Hysteria! It is not going to happen.

GRAHAM: How are you so sure?

VC: Because people like me are not going to let it happen!

GRAHAM: But you're dying, you old fool!

A silence.

Sorry, but I'm not going to apologise for that.

He pauses.

Probably your counterparts in the Soviet Union are dying too. The structure of matter, life itself is in the hands of foolish, sick, old men –

VC: Calm yourself, Graham.

GRAHAM: No, I won't calm myself! People like me keep on calming down in this bloody country and we do no end of harm. The work Leo has done and is now, in his confused way, trying to make amends for – we should protect it.

VC: Indeed. But is that not a good argument for putting the whole thing into the hands of the Ministry of Defence?

GRAHAM: Vice-Chancellor, have you not heard a word I have said? Did nothing that Leo and the girl did, in that rather puerile but desperate display in the garden, touch you at all?

VC: One is always pleased to see passion in the academic world, which is actually about academic work. Most of the passion round here goes on who is getting what salary.

GRAHAM: It is more a question of vision.

VC: Vision? Oh, vision. Now that can be tiresome –

GRAHAM: Vision of what a university can be –

VC: You're getting out of your depth, Graham. It's down to 'people like you' to run this place, not to ask what it is for.

GRAHAM (*low*): Disgraceful –

VC: What?

GRAHAM: That is a disgraceful remark!

VC: Oh don't be a pompous ass.

A silence.

GRAHAM: You know what our problem is here?

VC (*to himself*). I do, actually.

GRAHAM: Genius.

VC: Oh? Whose, yours? Sorry.

GRAHAM: We can't handle it. It seems the last place intellectual brilliance can prosper is a university. We must understand Leo Lehrer, if we can't, here, who will? We – must become like a monastery, in the dark ages. Keeping alive the secret of writing. Hiding the books in the cellars from barbarians.

With a flick of the head.

I propose we set up a Research Institute. We take no government or commercial money to finance it. We investigate Professor Lehrer's work – in secret. We find out of his fears are justified. Will his work lead to a knowledge of nature which will endanger nature itself? We answer that.

The VICE-CHANCELLOR, *with a sigh.*

VC: And if the answer is 'yes'?

GRAHAM: Then –

He pauses.

Then we bury it. In the cellars.

VC: Like an illuminated manuscript of the true gospel? Away from the gaze of the Viking hordes?

GRAHAM: Y – es. And we turn the university into a centre for Peace Studies. We win moral authority in the world –

The VICE-CHANCELLOR *with a sudden snort.*

VC: Ha ha! Sorry again. Like so many idealists you are so second rate, Graham, because you are hopelessly romantic.

He stretches himself in his chair.

Now I have to tell you, that Professor Lehrer's work is no longer our concern.

GRAHAM: What do you mean? It is our main concern –

VC: I said! Events! Running! Out of our hands!

GRAHAM: What have you done, you old fool, whom have you told –

VC: You are the fool.

He calls out.

Mr Dicks, would you come in?

TOM *comes into the room. He stands respectfully, smiling at* GRAHAM.

GRAHAM: I don't think a student should be present –

VC: Mr Dicks is a student, but that doesn't mean he is a student. He is a very bright fellow indeed. (*To* TOM.) Drink?

TOM: No thank you, Sir. May I –

VC: Do.

TOM: Bursar?

TOM *takes out a paper and pen and holds them out to* GRAHAM.

GRAHAM: ?

TOM: You can sign it in London, but –

He shrugs.

GRAHAM: London?

TOM: I've got to drive you down tonight.

A silence.

Better. This way, you'll be back lunchtime tomorrow. No one'll know you've been talked to. I mean, you've got no one at home at the moment, have you?

GRAHAM *hesitates.*

GRAHAM: No. Wh –

TOM: Official Secrets Act. You can sign it in London, but do it now and you'll feel happier, talking in the car.

GRAHAM: You sp – spy? On – your fellow students?

His voice cracks.

On your teachers?

TOM: I love good old squidgy England, don't you?

He pushes the paper and pen into GRAHAM*'s hands.*

Sign it Graham.

GRAHAM *does not move.*

VC: Sign it man. Why do the educated classes insist on seeing the world as something complex, when all the time it is brutally simple? Like – you are loyal to your country or you are not. And is England so bad? Walking in the autumn woods with your feet warm in your wellies. And your garden? House? Job? And a little malt whisky, late of a night?

He scoffs.

I mean, are you going to turn on all you believe in? Be photographed jumping the Berlin wall the wrong way – at your age?

They are all still. Then GRAHAM *scribbles fast, the paper held against his knee. He pushes the paper at* TOM, *who dangles car keys.*

TOM: OK. Off we go.

GRAHAM: I feel weakened.

TOM: Coffee and sandwiches in the car. Ok?

GRAHAM *looks at the* VICE-CHANCELLOR *then goes, quickly.* TOM *turns to the* VICE-CHANCELLOR.

All good gardening, Sir?

TOM *goes.*

VC: Garden. Grow. Achieve. Finance, build. Library extension, olympic standard swimming pool, opportunity, the young in one another's arms, brave new world.

He pauses.

Dust, all dust. And a sip of malt.

Scene Three: Treacheries.

Wood. Early afternoon. LEO *walking slowly, alone. He stops.*

LEO: You want to be quiet. Talk in a whisper. And what do you do? Open your mouth and scream.

He looks about him.

You want a swim in clear, cool, calm water. What do you do? Set off a tidal wave and drown all the swimmers in sight.

He pauses.

And here I am now. A walk in the woods, an afternoon among the trees. To think. Hey hey, careful man! A thinker round here, that's a human flame thrower. One thought, all the trees will be on fire.

He stops.

Oh shit. I have that feeling that they are watching you – when they are watching you.

He turns on the CYCLIST.

You have something to say to me?

CYCLIST: Have you to me?

LEO: No.

CYCLIST: Are you sure?

LEO: I keep on seeing you around. What is it with you?

CYCLIST: One strives to be a presence in the lives of the great and good.

LEO: Oh yeah? Why count me in their number

CYCLIST: Don't go modest on me, Mr American Scientist. An American affecting modesty really takes the pip.

LEO: What do you teach here?

CYCLIST: A load of rubbish called the History of Fine Art. The Government has so far failed to notice my department exists. When they do it is bound to be cut. Actually, it is not by accident I bump into you this afternoon. I have noticed you come to this wood now and then. No doubt for assignations of your choice.

LEO: What is that to you?

CYCLIST: Oh a great deal. You are a problem in my life, Mr American Scientist. For I do have something to say to you.

LEO (*to himself*): And you are going to say it, aren't you chummy.

The CYCLIST *pedals, glides and breaks near* LEO.

CYCLIST: You see, I doubt your prediction of highly radioactive isotopes from elements of low atomic weight.

LEO *stares.*

Within certain conditions of a unified field, which you postulate.

LEO *stares.*

Well I say 'I' doubt it, truer to say there are they who doubt it.

LEO: Why do they?

CYCLIST: Ah, now, there you have me by the short and curlies.

LEO: 'They' 'they', who is this 'they'?

CYCLIST: The word bothers you?

LEO: It splits my arse, Mr Fine Art.

CYCLIST: There is always a 'they', is there not, Mr Scientist?

LEO: That is my experience.

The CYCLIST *pauses.*

CYCLIST: You must have known this would be said to you, once in your distinguished career. Now it is being said. I give you the greetings of Professor Abelski and his wife Irena of the Leningrad Institute for the Advancement of Science. A delightful couple, though with something of a shared drink problem – I believe you met them in Los Angeles?

LEO: Oh wow.

CYCLIST: He has written you this letter.

He produces a long envelope from within his saddlebag. LEO *does not take it.*

LEO: Wow.

CYCLIST: A purely technical letter, detailing recent work he has done that may interest you. However Professor Abelski wishes you to know that the facilities of the Institute are at your disposal. The Socialist Peoples hope you will join them to work for world peace.

LEO: Wow.

He spins.

Wow wow.

He stops spinning.

I always thought you people would what, hit me with heavies in black coats, from a black limousine? Or a blond in the bathroom of an International Hotel, offering to suck me off? Not some freak who scours the English landscape for the Kremlin, on a push bike.

He laughs.

Oh wow.

He collects himself.

What do I do now? Weep? Mess my pants?

CYCLIST: That is up to you. We are all masters of our fate.

LEO: You believe that?

CYCLIST: Utterly. I get bloody irritated with intellectuals who do not.

LEO: I thought you commies were historical determinists.

CYCLIST: I don't think you want to get

into a dialectical discussion with me, sonny boy, I will have you for breakfast.

LEO: Bullshit.

CYCLIST (*to himself*): Oh dear oh dear, how your kind do bring out the worst in me.

LEO: Thinking about it – I'll mess my pants.

CYCLIST: That is a sort of reasoned response.

LEO: Reasoned? Oh yeah, you are an apostle of reason, being a communist. That's why I see you in the staff club, out of your head on eight pints a night.

CYCLIST: There is a strain, when you believe what I believe in this bloody country. I do not deny that. You take what relief is on offer, though it be pissy beer the profits from which fill the coffers of the Tory Party. But if personal habits are the matter of debate, shall we get onto yours? Cocaine and other men's wives?

LEO: I don't see there's any debate between us. I get the impression I am talking to a closed mind.

A silence.

CYCLIST: Yes, my mind is closed. I slammed the door on everything you represent, years ago. Ha! Thirty years in the Party, pushing pamphlets in the rain and now I do this. Probably the most important thing I will ever do in my life. You will find it bizarre, but I hope to retire in the Soviet Union. My wife and I are building a house there. We do it bit by bit, every summer holiday. Last trip, the border police found a load of copper piping T-joints under the back seat, for the plumbing. That cost me two hundred American dollars in backhanders. Next summer it'll be an English lavatory pan – that will be a heavy scene. You see, for all the horrors, the Socialist World is my 'they'. I know where I belong. Do you?

LEO (*to himself*): Belong. Belonging.

The CYCLIST *offers the letter.*

CYCLIST: Do you want this?

LEO *takes the letter.*

LEO: Just for the science.

CYCLIST: Yes of course, the science, the bloody blood-stained science.

He cycles a circle.

If you want me, I am always over the hedge.

He cycles off with a spurt of speed. LEO *holds the letter up, looking at it, then rips it open. There are thin sheets of paper. He flips through them, fixes on a passage then laughs.*

LEO: My God, are they that desperate?

GRAHAM, *drunk, and* VIRGINIA *come on at the back. They are in mid-argument,* VIRGINIA *holding his arm, he pulling away from her.*

GRAHAM: No, I bloody well will not!

VIRGINIA: Oh you will!

GRAHAM: I will or I will not do what I will!

VIRGINIA: When, Graham?

GRAHAM: When I will.

They struggle. LEO, *aside, waving the letter.*

LEO: Hey hey, a bribe from the East with promise of glory in history. And here comes the West, with sex and drink and the bitchiness I know and love. It is a very tasty world.

He laughs.

GRAHAM: You laughing at me?

VIRGINIA: Go away, Leo.

GRAHAM: He is laughing at me.

VIRGINIA: Please Leo..

GRAHAM: I want to know why your lover is laughing at me.

VIRGINIA (*to* LEO): We are negotiating the sale of our house. Or at least I am. Please have the decency to go away and leave us alone –

GRAHAM: Can't walk away from each other!

VIRGINIA: Oh no, no.

She walks a distance away and stops.

LEO: Where you been, Graham? I called you.

VIRGINIA: We would all like to know where he has been. And, indeed, where he thinks he is now.

GRAHAM: All right all right, you want my fingernails? Take 'em.

Offering his fingers.

One to ten, all the way!

LEO: Is he smashed?

VIRGINIA: Am I my husband's keeper?

LEO: What's the matter, Graham?

GRAHAM: Matter, matter, atomic matter, with me?

He giggles.

LEO: You've got to get over me and her.

Indicating VIRGINIA.

I mean, old man, it was only sex. We're all happy dogs in the park getting up each other, why make a big scene?

VIRGINIA: How charming, how beautiful, how lyrical. If there is going to be talk from the male jockstrap I am going –

GRAHAM: No.

He blocks her way. A silence.

No. I – was down in London. All night.

A silence.

Taken, to London. And questioned. (*To* LEO.) About you. So please. Neither of you – go. Or speak loudly to me any more. I –

He looks down.

Have been badly frightened.

LEO: Jesus Christ.

GRAHAM: As a young man said to me, last night – 'We are all locked together in a room, no one can leave!' (*To himself.*) Had a feeling he'd said that to others before me. It had the feel of a truth worn smooth. (*To* LEO.) He said it to me in a car, on the motorway, I looked at the car door, thought 'Can I throw myself out, like in the films? Roll away in the dark, to fanfares . . .'

VIRGINIA: Graham –

GRAHAM: No, don't touch me! I am holy. Member of a holy band. Who have been canonised to the sainthood of our times – those who have been in the hands of the secret police. English, but nevertheless, secret police.

He laughs.

Know what? They're all old Etonians. It really is amazing to discover your country is a totalitarian state, run by old Etonians. (*To himself.*) In a big room with carpets and a big fireplace.

VIRGINIA: I don't think this country is a totalitarian state, it's just a squalid mess. I'm sorry, but run by men like you, Graham.

GRAHAM: Think I'm exaggerating? That's because they've not touched you yet, 'darling'. (*At* LEO.) Or him. Oh no, not the glamorous prize-winner. It's decent little runts like me that get the horrors.

LEO: If you fool around with a secret of the universe, the local cops are bound to call. What do you expect, old man?

GRAHAM: I do not expect to be interrogated. About you. Threatened! I mean, we've all got our lives and they really are rather p – precious to us. I mean, I will go to the wall with the rest, under the mushroom cloud, but alone? With young men in sm – smart suits, sneering at me?

LEO: It is cruel to say this, Graham – but you had better tell me what you told them.

GRAHAM: I had better not.

He looks at his hands.

No, I told them the lot. Your hands look the same. Air, going up your nose, feels the same. I am so scared.

LEO: You told them –

GRAHAM: Yes yes yes! The rumours about you in America, you and the girl's work, the rumours in the staff club about your druggy habits, all that you've been up to. Yes! And –

He pauses.

You and her. (*Meaning* VIRGINIA.) Yes!

A silence.

Utter betrayal. Ut – ter nakedness. What I regret is that I was not stripped naked, put up against a wall, in a filthy cellar, cold freezing water, I am ashamed that I was not.

LEO (*low*): You little shit.

GRAHAM: More of that, please, if you can. It is very sweet to me. Leo –

He pauses.

It's the girl they want. You, they think they can handle. Perhaps they're confident your pleasures will bring you to heel? But little Gillian – oh dear, the chip off a fallen star, the meteorite, your little skirt with the goods, eh?

He giggles.

She really bothers 'em. Female, genius, state secrets? Chaps know chaps will, in the end, do what chaps should. Shut up. Pull together. But little Gilly? Different animal. Not got a chap's tackle between the legs, chaps get very jumpy indeed. For all I know, when they find her they'll put a bullet in the back of her neck. Tell me where she is.

He pauses.

Friend.

He slurs.

I feel disgusting. I studied William Blake, revolutionary visionary. I think I'd better sit d –

He plomps down.

LEO: I've no idea where Gilly is, tell them that, no idea.

GRAHAM: Please, you must. While I was being questioned – I wet myself, out of fear. That is not an English experience – I never want it in my life again.

LEO: I told you old son, she's gone.

GRAHAM: I have destroyed myself for you. Argued for you. Do this for me.

LEO: How can I?

GRAHAM: They won't do anything to her. Just take her in hand. Rap her over the wrists.

VIRGINIA: Steal her mathematics?

GRAHAM: Just nail her down to the floor! It'll be all very British. They'll give her a grant or something. But one way or another, nailed to the floor she will be! We must all be nailed to the floor! Where we belong!

LEO: I can't do anything for you, Graham. As you once said, our cause is purity.

GRAHAM: He refers to his science. His true love. Quote!
'You love the world that I hate.
Thy heaven's doors are my hell gate'.
That's Blake.

He hiccups.

More or less. Which gate does your science go in, eh Leo?

LEO: You podgy little Englishman, what are you moaning about? You think that purity, a pure thought, a pure line through the mindmoil will not cost? I've had the gremlins out of the wall for me, too. Take my advice. Carry no baggage. No friends. Fuck if you must, but don't make love. Be light.

GRAHAM: Ha!

A silence.

Ha. I could never take that about you. Your freedom and b – beauty. The person who throws off all human feeling is *so* free, so beautiful, real people like me, we bumblers, we sweaters, we can't handle the chaos. Therefore –

He struggles to his feet.

I am ditching you. I am withdrawing my love. Divorce my wife, name you –

VIRGINIA: Oh! Thank you very much.

GRAHAM: And I will have you out of the university in a year. Batter my way, back up. I'll be Vice-Chancellor by the time I'm sixty. If I be not burnt to a crisp in your Third World War. Eh?

He looks from one to the other. They do not laugh.

Eh? Eh?

He lurches away.

LEO: See you at the gate.

GRAHAM *stops, not looking at* LEO.

GRAHAM: Don't think so. I'm going to Heaven. 'Friend'. So sod the both of you.

He lurches away and goes off.

VIRGINIA: Do you enjoy effortless, personal cruelty?

LEO: Yup.

VIRGINIA: Cold – as – ice.

LEO: That is me.

VIRGINIA: Your cause is purity.

He looks at his watch.

Seeing you destroy my husband in that cause – well, I suppose it was an interesting insight into the men's locker room. The patterns on the wall look quite pretty – 'til you realise they're made with blood. What are you up to, Leo?

LEO: How d'you mean?

VIRGINIA: You're waiting for someone.

Nothing from LEO.

I know it can't be the girl.

LEO: How do you know that?

VIRGINIA: Because I am hiding her.

A silence.

With a friend. Never mind who. Should I have told you?

LEO: Dunno.

A silence.

You didn't tell your husband.

VIRGINIA: To put him out of his agony.

LEO: No.

VIRGINIA: No.

LEO: See what it does to you, Vee? You too grow cold.

He pauses.

Is she OK?

VIRGINIA: What you mean is 'are the mathematics OK?' The little squiggles. The 'ideas'. Has she gone off her head, left them on a bus, in a railway station ladies loo, put them in a bottle and thrown them in the sea?

She pauses.

The mathematics are OK. As for Gilly, she thinks you are a hero.

Nothing from LEO.

I said she –

LEO: I heard you.

VIRGINIA: She wants to see you.

Nothing from LEO.

I said she –

LEO (*shouts*). You did!

A silence.

VIRGINIA: What are you doing Leo, why are you waiting here while we all wash in blood around you? You won't see her?

Nothing from LEO.

You taught her.

LEO: It was never my intention to teach anyone.

VIRGINIA: Oh?

LEO: Or to remake the world at large. All I am is a kid who was in love with numbers. The bitch with numbers is – they add up. And the totals are not wholly numerical. They are a British kid running out of a garden. You. Graham out of his mind. Some room with carpets in London. Letters from the East. Threats from the West. Trees on fire. But what is all that to do with me? I feel like a singer, who sings a note in innocence and all the glass in the windows smashes. Is the consequence of what I think down to me or not? I say – not. I am sick of being some kind of moralist by default – all because I was in love with numbers.

VIRGINIA *stares at him. Upstage the* VICE-CHANCELLOR *comes on with* TOM, *who stands a few yards away. The light is now that of a golden late afternoon.* VIRGINIA *turns and sees the* VICE-CHANCELLOR. *He smiles.*

VC: Good evening, Virginia.

VIRGINIA *whirls on* LEO, *who does not look at her.*

LEO (*low*): Just go home. Run a bath. Put on the TV. Then, whatever you've got in the house to blow your mind, use it.

VIRGINIA (*low*): You American bastard. What have they offered you?

She pauses, then turns and runs off. The VICE-CHANCELLOR *and* TOM *come down to* LEO, *slowly,* TOM *keeping his distance.*

LEO: I want you to think very carefully how you speak to me, because I may suddenly throw up on you.

VC: Understood, Professor Lehrer.

LEO: This –

He takes a key out of his pocket.

Is a key to a locker on Birmingham Railway Station, there you will find all the material, from me, from the girl, with a breakdown of the work you will also find in the university's computer.

VC: Ah.

A silence. Then LEO *throws the key into the air.* TOM *takes a few steps back and catches it. The* VC *and* TOM *relax.*

You –

He pauses.

Bumped into our resident red mole earlier this afternoon.

He pauses.

Dear old Cliff Jones, you know he is trying to build a house somewhere in the Urals?

He laughs.

A real local character is Cliff. Of course I am doing everything to stop his department being cut, but – Fine Art? In these harsh, utilitarian times? Particularly when it's Fine Art run by an alcoholic Marxist-Leninist –

LEO (*shouts*). All right! (*Low.*) All right.

He takes out the letter and holds it up. TOM *comes forward and takes it, deliberately.*

TOM: Do you know where the girl is?

LEO: I said be very careful how you talk to me –

VC: There are –

He pauses.

Her parents to think of. The university is responsible for the children in its care –

LEO: No!

A silence.

VC: No matter. All will be well. Now that we are at peace. I know you want nothing said. An act of conscience is a lonely thing. Best resolved at the soul's still centre? All I will say is –

LEO *closes his eyes.*

I find it rather wonderful that an exile from your country, has given us all a lesson in patriotism.

He holds his hand out to shake. LEO *vomits, crouching.*

My dear fellow –

TOM *touches the* VICE-CHANCELLOR*'s arm and shakes his head. They walk away. The* VICE-CHANCELLOR *stops and looks back at* LEO.

VC: One is tempted to say 'And we did not even have to show him the instruments of torture'. Young man, I will buy you a drink in the staff club.

They go off, the VICE-CHANCELLOR *helped by* TOM*'s arm.* LEO *alone. The stage darkens. Moonlight.* LEO, *still crouching, sniffs cocaine. He grunts, he breathes deeply, he coughs.* GILLY, VIRGINIA *and* ANDREA *come on. They do not see* LEO.

GILLY: Leo? Leo?

VIRGINIA: Gilly this is wrong –

GILLY: He'll be here.

ANDREA: With policemen watching –

GILLY: Leo?

VIRGINIA: God I hate being frightened, I hate it.

GILLY: He – will – be – here!

ANDREA: Aren't you sick of dangerous men by now?

GILLY: He's not dangerous just too clever, too bloody clever by half!

She runs forward.

Where are you? Clever teacher!

VIRGINIA: We've got to stop her –

ANDREA: Just let her, let her.

GILLY: Let me see you, clever man, clever, clever man.

She sees LEO *and approaches him.*

Why?

She pauses.

Why?

She pauses.

Why?

LEO: Let – us – say –

He pauses.

That I have exchanged a walk-on part in the war, for a lead role in a cage.

He giggles, coughs.

Isn't that from a pop-song somewhere? Y'know, you grasp at splinters. As they fly past you in the air –

He wipes his nose with his sleeve.

GILLY: You've given it all to them?

He stares at her.

LEO: Yeah, 'the discovery', the 'great work', yeah I've given them the whole kerboodle. You want some of this?

The cocaine. GILLY *ignores it.*

GILLY: You showed me how they can make new weapons. Out of what you and I wrote down, on thirty bits of paper. You were brilliant, in six hours, you showed me the physics, out of pure numbers – like a terrible web, spinning out. When you finished I screamed, I screamed, I still am screaming inside. And after doing that to me, you turn round, like a traitor – (*Low.*) I believed in you.

LEO: Mistake. If there is one thing we have to do, it's to learn not to believe in each other.

GILLY: No?

LEO: No. None of us can take the strain.

GILLY (*shouts*): Tell me why you did it!

LEO (*shouts*): Because!

He shakes his head, he blinks his eyes.

Because I despair. Right? I despair. That is the personal bullshit.

He pauses.

As for the intellectual bullshit – the ideas, Gillian. The ideas do not love us. I have come to the conclusion that all the investigations into the atom, discoveries, calculations, formulations, nearer and nearer to the description of the force of nature – the scientific quest of the century – is fundamentally malign. All the technology that has flowed from it, atomic fission, power stations to bombs, the actual material – is malign.

He laughs.

Get your head round this one, philosopher. What if the most *un*natural thing our species can do, is to understand nature itself? Malignity! In the ideas, in the idea of the ideas. If I were religious – and thank the fuck I'm not – I'd start talking about evil.

VIRGINIA *and* ANDREA *come on at the back.*

VIRGINIA: Gilly?

They see her and stop.

LEO: Yup! If I were the Pope, I think I would announce that we are forbidden to know the true nature of gravity, electromagnetism and the nuclear forces. But – too late, holiness. We're never going to dig that knowledge out of our lives, out of our thoughts, out of our machines. Yup! As Pope I think I'd burn myself at the stake. Did you say you wanted some of this?

The cocaine. She hits him once, very deliberately on the side of the head. He laughs.

VIRGINIA: Gilly, they're probably watching him. Come on.

GILLY: Thank you – for teaching me – the physics.

Near tears, she runs to VIRGINIA *and* ANDREA. *They go off quickly.*

LEO: What about you, then? Walk-on part in the war?

He looks about him.

Gilly?

He pauses.

Where are you?

He pauses.

Where you gone?

He pauses.

(*Slurred.*) Well am I right or not? Look –

He pauses.

Let's calculate it through 'til come the rosy dawn.

He pauses.

Float away, come the rosy dawn, do some maths.

He pauses.

This time you show me, eh? You pass me the poison. Teach the teacher.

He pauses.

Eh? (*Low.*) I need you, student. Where are you?

Scene Four: Embassy.

In the blackout, the low electrical hum, building up to a screech, then a second of silence –

The lights come on, brilliant all over the stage. The hum returns.

GILLY *walks forward. She is dressed in soiled, outdoor clothes. She bends under the weight of a large hiker's back-pack, messily put together, a rolled sleeping bag hangs from it.*

GILLY'S MOTHER *walks with her, played by* VIRGINIA, *who is in lumpy, winter clothes, a middle-aged woman's coat, holding the pink umbrella to obscure her face.*

GILLY: Don't go on, Mum. I got to get up this hill.

MOTHER: I don't know why you hurt me and Daddy –

GILLY: Why do you always call him 'Daddy'?

MOTHER: Living in filth and dirt. I worry so much about how you live –

GILLY: I worry about you too, Mum.

MOTHER: Like that time I found pills under your pillow and was worried sick you were on drugs –

GILLY: They were aspirins, Mum. I was twelve. I had my first period.

MOTHER: Things I don't want brought into the house. Like that poster on your wall of a bomb going off –

GILLY: But the poster means don't let the bomb go off!

GILLY *slips the back-pack off.*

Please, I'm so tired.

MOTHER: You're our only child. We had you late. You don't realise. When the back extension roof went and damp got in I couldn't sleep for months.

GILLY: I'm tired.

She sits, leaning against the back-pack.

MOTHER: All the terrible things in the world. What if Daddy got sick? If we lost the house we'd have to sleep in a hole in the ground, all because of you.

GILLY *closes her eyes.*

GILLY: Don't want you to live in a hole in the ground, Mum.

MOTHER: Blowing people up, going to prison, men in the parks and little girls, guns, pornography, oh, that poster looks communist, Gilly, Daddy's ever so upset.

GILLY: Sorry Mum, did I bring the nuclear bomb indoors?

VIRGINIA: Gilly wake up!

GILLY: But the bomb's in you, Mum.

VIRGINIA: Gilly!

GILLY: In you! It'll go off in you!

VIRGINIA: Gilly, for godsake!

GILLY *wakes up with a start.*

VIRGINIA *lowers the umbrella.*

The light changes to a drab, London afternoon. It is raining. At the back, the dull, smeared green of a park. The hum changes to the sound of traffic.

Don't go to sleep. There's a policeman looking at you.

GILLY: My mum never wanted it in the house.

VIRGINIA: Gilly, get up.

GILLY: Oh yes.

She stands, stiffly.

VIRGINIA: You just plomped down on the pavement and went to sleep –

GILLY: Yes.

VIRGINIA: We're so tired, so –

ANDREA *runs on.*

ANDREA: I got inside. There was a man in a shabby suit, in front of a TV screen. Opening letters. I couldn't make him understand.

VIRGINIA: What did he say?

ANDREA: 'No.'

VIRGINIA: 'Niet.'

She scoffs.

ANDREA: It doesn't look like the Russian Embassy. Just any old big house, behind any old hedge. Except for the cameras on the walls.

GILLY: We've got to see him.

VIRGINIA: They are not going to pay any attention to us Gilly. Look at us. Three tramps. Cranks in the rain.

ANDREA: Gilly wants to do this. Let her.

VIRGINIA: Madness.

GILLY: We've got to see the ambassador.

VIRGINIA: A naive gesture. And I'm not even sure it's right –

ANDREA: Shut up Vee.

VIRGINIA: All right, I know I am the older woman on this escapade. I mean, I think she was dreaming I am her mother!

GILLY: I'll go in.

ANDREA: The man in the shabby suit told me to leave. They won't let you in.

GILLY: Then I'll post it through the letterbox.

VIRGINIA: Oh for crying out loud.

GILLY: It's in my back-pack –

VIRGINIA: Don't –

But GILLY *is pulling at the back-pack.*

That policeman's looking at us again. He'll think you've got a bomb in there.

ANDREA: Gilly does think she's got a bomb in there.

GILLY *pulls out a big envelope and her binder.*
She pauses.

GILLY: I'm doing this because there must be no more secrets.

A silence.

I won't be a mo.

She runs off.

VIRGINIA: Look at us. We're like refugees.

ANDREA: That's what we are.

VIRGINIA: No country?

She laughs.

The anarchy, the squalor. I never thought 'protest' would be this – grubby.

ANDREA: Who was it said 'The only country I have is the people I love'?

VIRGINIA (*low*): Come on, come on.

A silence.

Refugees.

A laugh.

But what's the war? Against men, against the East, against the West, even against ourselves? Or just against death, jolly old mother Death?

ANDREA: Father Death?

GILLY *runs back on.*

GILLY: Plop. Just like that. There was a cat, sitting up in the ivy, by the steps. She blinked at me and said 'Meow! What have you done?' 'Done something at least, my dear' I said.

A blackout and –

Scene Five: Peace moves.

The Bach Theme is heard, played, undistorted, by the violin.

In the blackout the sound of strong wind and rain begins and grows.

The lights come up to an ugly, grey dawn before layers of wire fences that recede into the distance. The wire on the fences rattles and hums in the strong wind.

Large sheets of mud-streaked polythene flap on the stage before the fences.

Four POLICEMEN, *played anonymously by the* VICE-CHANCELLOR, GRAHAM, TOM *and* CYCLIST *actors, stand amongst the polythene sheets. They are in bad weather capes and each has a walky talky.*

The SKELETON VIOLINIST *sits to one side, playing. A woman – she wears a fisherman's hat against the bad weather.*

VIRGINIA *and* ANDREA *are moving plastic bags and rucksacks about from beneath the polythene, taking no notice of the* POLICEMEN.

The noise of the wind, that is of wind machines in the wings, the rattling of the fences and flapping of the polythene, is almost too much for speech to be heard.

LEO *and* GILLY, *both well wrapped-up, are downstage. She carries the pink umbrella, again blown inside out, and a large cake tin. She is struggling to open the tin.*

GILLY: My mum sent me a cake!

LEO: You what?

GILLY: Cake! Can you open it?

LEO: Yeah, cake –

GILLY: I expect it's bloody sponge!

She holds the tin, he pulls at the lid.

Do you want to see Vee? She's over there.

LEO: I turned up. Had no idea you were here. Don't you get pneumonia?

GILLY: What?

LEO: Pneumonia.

GILLY: Never healthier.

LEO: Here we go!

The cake tin lid comes off.

GILLY: I've done more work! On the equations! You?

LEO: Yeah, it don't stop–

GILLY: In my head, all the time – hey it's fruit!

LEO: There's a note – hey!

He stops it blowing away. He gives GILLY *the note. She turns against the wind and reads it.*

LEO: Have the planes come in?

GILLY *laughs at the note.*

They said in the press, anyday, the planes come in.

GILLY: My bloody mother says she's proud of me and sent me a cake! My bloody mother!

LEO: This is what I done recently!

He takes a brown envelope from beneath his coat. In the distance, the sound of planes approaching.

GILLY: I got something too, here!

She zips open the front of her coat. A binder. She holds it out.

New binder! The planes with the missiles will be Galaxy transporters. We're going through the wire, onto the runway. Swop?

They swop envelope and binder. The noise of planes and wind rising. They laugh. They embrace. ANDREA *and* VIRGINIA *turn and run at the wire,* VIRGINIA *making a hold for* ANDREA*'s foot. She climbs up the wire. The* POLICEMEN *run at them. They freeze,* ANDREA*'s fingers in the wire, the* POLICEMEN *crowded in,* LEO *and* GILLY *embracing.*

The lights go down. The noise ceases. There are a few notes further from the Bach Theme.

Methuen New Theatrescripts

*Published in the Royal Court Writers Series
†Published in the RSC Playtexts Series
††Published in the Women's Playhouse Plays Series

SAMBA
by Michael Abbensetts

EAST-WEST & IS UNCLE JACK A CONFORMIST?
by Andrey Amalrik

*BURIED INSIDE EXTRA
by Thomas Babe

*THE LUCKY CHANCE
by Aphra Behn

DEREK & CHORUSES FROM AFTER THE ASSASSINATIONS
HUMAN CANNON
WAR PLAYS
by Edward Bond

SORE THROATS & SONNETS OF LOVE AND OPPOSITION
*THE GENIUS
by Howard Brenton
THIRTEENTH NIGHT & A SHORT SHARP SHOCK!
by Howard Brenton (*A Short Sharp Shock!* written with Tony Howard)
SLEEPING POLICEMEN
by Howard Brenton and Tunde Ikoli

†MOLIÈRE
by Mikhail Bulgakov (in a version by Dusty Hughes)

†MONEY
by Edward Bulwer-Lytton

RETURN TO THE FORBIDDEN PLANET
by Bob Carlton

*THE SEAGULL
by Anton Chekov (in a version by Thomas Kilroy)

FEN
SOFT COPS
by Caryl Churchill

SHONA, LUNCH GIRLS, THE SHELTER
by Tony Craze, Ron Hart, Johnnie Quarrell

WRECKERS
TEENDREAMS
by David Edgar

*MASTERPIECES
by Sarah Daniels

†THE BODY
by Nick Darke

TORCH SONG TRILOGY
by Harvey Fierstein

†OUR FRIENDS IN THE NORTH
by Peter Flannery

*OTHER WORLDS
by Robert Holman

*RAT IN THE SKULL
by Ron Hutchinson

†PEER GYNT
by Henrik Ibsen (translated by David Rudkin)

*INSIGNIFICANCE
CRIES FROM THE MAMMAL HOUSE
by Terry Johnson

FROZEN ASSETS
SUS
BASTARD ANGEL
by Barrie Keeffe

*NOT QUITE JERUSALEM
by Paul Kember

*BORDERLINE
by Hanif Kureishi

TOUCHED
*TIBETAN INROADS
THE RAGGED TROUSERED PHILANTHROPISTS
MOVING PICTURES: Four Plays (*Moving Pictures; Seachange; Stars; Strive*)
by Stephen Lowe

PROGRESS & HARD FEELINGS
by Doug Lucie

LAVENDER BLUE & NOLI ME TANGERE
by John Mackendrick

THICK AS THIEVES
WELCOME HOME, RASPBERRY, THE LUCKY ONES
by Tony Marchant

†A NEW WAY TO PAY OLD DEBTS
by Philip Massinger

NICE, RUM AN' COCA COLA & WELCOME HOME JACKO
PLAY MAS, INDEPENDENCE & MEETINGS
by Mustapha Matura

LUNATIC AND LOVER
by Michael Meyer

*OPERATION BAD APPLE
*AN HONOURABLE TRADE
by G.F.Newman

SALONIKA
REAL ESTATE
by Louise Page

ONE FOR THE ROAD
by Harold Pinter

STRAWBERRY FIELDS
SHOUT ACROSS THE RIVER
AMERICAN DAYS
THE SUMMER PARTY
FAVOURITE NIGHTS & CAUGHT ON A TRAIN
RUNNERS & SOFT TARGETS
BREAKING THE SILENCE
by Stephen Poliakoff

BRIMSTONE AND TREACLE
by Dennis Potter

†THE TIME OF YOUR LIFE
by William Saroyan

††SPELL NUMBER 7
by Ntozake Shange

MY DINNER WITH ANDRÉ & MARIE AND BRUCE
by Wallace Shawn (*My Dinner with André* written with André Gregory)

LIVE THEATRE: Four Plays for Young People
by C.P.Taylor

BAZAAR & RUMMAGE, GROPING FOR WORDS & WOMBERANG
*THE GREAT CELESTIAL COW
by Sue Townsend

PLAYS BY WOMEN VOL ONE
(*Vinegar Tom* by Caryl Churchill; *Dusa, Fish, Stas and Vi* by Pam Gems; *Tissue* by Louise Page; *Aurora Leigh* by Michelene Wandor)

PLAYS BY WOMEN VOL TWO
(*Rites* by Maureen Duffy; *Letters Home* by Rose Leiman Goldemberg; *Trafford Tanzi* by Claire Luckham; *Find Me* by Olwen Wymark)
PLAYS BY WOMEN VOL THREE
(*Aunt Mary* by Pam Gems; *Red Devils* by Debbie Horsfield; *Blood Relations* by Sharon Pollock; *Time Pieces* by Lou Wakefield and The Women's Theatre Group)
PLAYS BY WOMEN VOL FOUR
(*Objections to Sex and Violence* by Caryl Churchill; *Rose's Story* by Grace Daley; *Blood and Ice* by Liz Lochhead; *Pinball* by Alison Lyssa)
by Michelene Wandor (Ed.)

†CLAY
by Peter Whelan

THE NINE NIGHT & RITUAL BY WATER
by Edgar White

RENTS
LENT
by David Wilcox

GAY PLAYS
(*Submariners* by Tom McClenaghan; *The Green Bay Tree* by Mordaunt Shairp; *Passing By* by Martin Sherman; *Accounts* by Michael Wilcox)
by Michael Wilcox (Ed.)

SUGAR AND SPICE & TRIAL RUN
W.C.P.C.
by Nigel Williams

*THE GRASS WIDOW
by Snoo Wilson

HAS 'WASHINGTON' LEGS & DINGO
by Charles Wood

CUSTOM OF THE COUNTRY
by Nicholas Wright